It's HOW You Say It™

EFFECTIVE BUSINESS COMMUNICATION SKILLS

by Barbara Teicher

Warning/Disclaimer

No part of this book may be used or reproduced in any written, electronic, recorded, photocopied or any other manner without written permission of the author. The exception would be in case of brief quotations embodied in critical articles and reviews and pages where permission is specifically granted by All Aboard publishing or the author, Barbara Teicher.

Although every precaution has been taken to verify the accuracy of the information contained herein, the author and publisher assume no responsibility for any errors or omissions. No liability is assumed for damages that may result from the use of information contained within.

Cover Design: Brad Springer and Barbara Teicher
Editor: Karen L. Anderson, KarenLAnderson@kc.rr.com
Artist: Brad Springer

Editor's Note: The author uses contractions to provide a conversational tone and the synesis device of a plural pronoun referring to a singular person as a gender-inclusive reference.

It's HowYou Say It. Copyright © 2014 by Barbara Teicher.
All rights reserved.

ISBN-10: 1499112394
ISBN 13: 9781499112399
Library of Congress Control Number: 2014906928
CreateSpace Independent Publishing Platform
North Charleston, South Carolina

Dedication

This book is dedicated to my wonderful family:

Adam, who is still my hero and heartbeat after 21 years of marriage.

Our beautiful daughter, Hannah, whose wonderful heart and smile light up my days.

Our faithful companions: Shadow, our loving protector, who's waiting for us on the other side of the rainbow bridge, and Aspen, our Kansas tornado, who distributes her golden fur on absolutely everything in our home.

And to God and His son for loving me, saving me and showing me to take my work and the people I serve seriously, but never myself!

Acknowledgments

This book would not have been completed if it weren't for the diligence, time and great talent of my editor, Karen L. Anderson. Her insights, suggestions, kindness and expertise made the editing process a wonderful learning experience.

Table of Contents

Dedication	iii
Acknowledgments	v
Preface	ix
Introduction	xi
Part I: Laying Tracks	1
Chapter One: Communication Components	3
Chapter Two: Communication Barriers	17
Part II: Avoiding Train Wrecks and Staying on Track	35
Chapter Three: The Five "Disconnects"	37
Chapter Four: The 6-Step "It's HOW You Say It"™ Principle for Effective Communication	61
Part III: Navigating the Stations & Sidetracks to Reach Your Destination	89
Chapter Five: True Leadership - How to Become the Difference	91

Summary	**121**
About the Author	**123**
To Order	**125**
Resources	**127**

Preface

It's HOW You Say It. Very true. There are many different cars that make up this complex train of relationships, projects, equipment, and technology we call effective business communication.

This book is divided into three parts. Where you start reading may depend upon where you are in your leadership journey. Part I, Chapters I and II, is for emerging managers. If you are fairly new to management or supervision, you'll want to read this book and start your ride at the very beginning. Background and history in these earlier chapters are important and contain foundational information and research that shines the light on the reasons for those train wrecks we sometimes experience in business communication.

If you are a seasoned manager, and the concepts in Part I are familiar to you, you'll want to start at the beginning of Part II which couples Chapters III and IV to give you information, science and skills for the wild ride through management.

If you are an officer or seasoned leader, you may want to begin your journey in Part III, which is Chapter V. Although you're now the engineer of your fast-moving train, remember you may have emerging leaders, managers or new supervisors on your teams who you will want to mentor and help switch tracks as appropriate. Afterall, what difference does it make to be the first one to the station if your train only has you on it?

Train Metaphor	Effective Business Communication
Tracks & Infrastructure	Business Plans, Communication Technology (blogging, websites, smart phones, social media)
Engineer	Business Leader
Engine/Locomotive	Vision/Mission
Fuel	Passion, Motivation
Cars	Projects
Caboose	The Last Car on the Train
Ticket Agents	Client/Customer Service & Sales Reps
Passengers	Internal & External Clients, Work Teams
Cargo	Products, Services, Initiatives, Processes, Work Environment
Conductors	Mid-level Managers
Maintenance & Operations Crews	Work Teams, Technicians
Regulators	Compliance Officer
Stations	Milestones
Sidetracks	Tangents/Delays
Destination	Goal Attainment

Why this book and not others? This book is a blend of experiential, as well as empirical data I have accumulated during my 25 plus years working with and developing corporate America's leading officers and managers. I have supported these concepts and principles with scientific research from some of the most well-respected sources in the country.

At the end of each chapter will be two sections: The Science of It All and All Aboard. These sections will contain both scientific data or research to support its content as well as application activities to reinforce the chapter's learnings.

ALL ABOARD

Introduction

Many years ago I became intrigued by the way people **communicate** with each other - not the way they talk to each other, but the actual messages they feel they are sending and the disconnects with the way they, themselves, are often perceived.

Has it ever happened that someone takes offense at something you've said, and you have no idea why? Maybe the opposite happens, and you've taken offense at someone else's words only to hear, "I think you took that the wrong way." Why did you take it the "wrong" way?

Differences in existing personal and business relationships, as well as how well we know someone, can mean differences in the way we talk and relate to each other, too. What about those people you haven't met before? Why does there seem to be a strong disconnection with some, an instant feeling that this may not be a relationship you'll want to grow and protect, and yet, you have an almost instant bonding with others?

The way you say something can be more important and powerful than the words you actually use. The intent behind the words we try to convey, though, may be in opposition to the message being perceived. They are often not in sync at all.... Why?

It's difficult to navigate these differences, whether speaking with the CEO or speaking with the neighbor next door. We address people, depending upon our relationship with them, in specific ways.

It's not enough to choose our words carefully. Words themselves don't have the impact the delivery does.

After 25 years in corporate America, interacting and working with leaders from the CEO's of world-recognized Fortune 50 - Fortune 500 companies, to the entry level positions in both large and small businesses, I know it is evident that it's not just what you say, *"It's HOW You Say It."*™

The information found in this book will give you insight into the nuances in communication, and, I will share with you the secrets of understanding how to say your words so that the intention of your message and conversation is the same as the one being perceived by the other person you are talking with.

PART I
LAYING TRACKS

Part One includes Chapters I and II. This was written for the new manager or supervisor who may not be aware of the many different ways they communicate messages. Because of this, messages may be sent unconsciously that are misperceived often causing challenges in the workplace.

As a new manager, building strong, foundational management skills is critical.

A railroad company has to have a strong track laid and solid switching stations for trains to carry their cargo seamlessly from track to track in order to arrive safely at their destinations with that cargo intact. A leader must also lay down strong foundational management skills to move seamlessly between the numerous tasks, projects and varied responsibilities they carry too in order to arrive safely with their teams in tact when chugging towards the company's goals.

CHAPTER ONE
Communication Components

No romantic comedy and no sitcom (situational comedy) can work without miscommunication and misunderstanding -- from *"I Love Lucy"* to *"Murphy Brown"* to *"The Office."* Each script presents its characters with situations in which someone's insecurity is fed by misperceptions. This comedy of errors also occurs in households and offices across the nation because it's not just what you say, "It's **HOW** You Say It."™

What are the varied components that make up communication? Scientists all over the globe study this question. A better question may be "What makes up effective communication?" There are just as many varied thoughts on this as there are answers.

First, we need to look into the individual components of effective communication. What is business communication, for example? Is there a difference in the way we communicate in a business setting as opposed to a personal setting? What is meant by non-verbal communication? Communication isn't just one modality. So let's take a look at several areas of interpersonal communication in business and where people may struggle. You may not even know you're struggling. The challenges you're having with others in your work environment let you know something's not right, even if you can't put a finger on what it is.

In 1983, Howard Gardner's *Frames of Mind: The Theory of Multiple Intelligences* introduced the idea of Multiple Intelligences which included both interpersonal intelligence (the capacity to understand the intentions, motivations and desires of other people) and intrapersonal intelligence (the capacity to understand one's self, to appreciate one's feelings, fears and motivations).

For the purpose of this chapter, the objective will be to concentrate on the components of communication that are most common. From these, we'll take a look at the challenges of these typical components in communication. We'll also look at what makes them effective, and the wide differences they represent, depending upon the person with whom you may be engaged in conversation.

In personal settings, as in a business setting, there are also many aspects of communication that are not visible. How do you know what you may be doing that's sending a signal you are unaware of? Let's look at a high level into some of the initial components that make up this mystery called communication.

1. The Eyes Have It
2. Your Voice
3. Posture, Body Language and Gestures

1. The Eyes Have It

It's possible to have an entire conversation with your eyes alone. In a business setting, what you are looking at, what you are NOT looking at, and the message your eye contact is sending, can have an extreme impact. It can give you credibility, take that credibility away or leave others feeling as though you are totally disconnected... all without your awareness. You've probably heard the saying, "The eyes are

PART I   LAYING TRACKS

the windows to the soul." If you're talking with someone you're not really fond of, that can be a scary thought!

Without words, eyes can communicate agreement, acceptance, happiness, anger, mistrust and even disconnection. Eyes can move you to action or keep you glued to your seat.

When our daughter was very young, she had done something that had warranted a "time out." I looked at her, and before I had said anything, she said to me very seriously, "Mama, did you have to go to school for that?" "For what?" I asked her. "To learn," she said as she looked so very intently at me, "the Look!" She is now 19. She laughs and says she still sees "The Mom Look."

When I worked for a very large telecommunications company, I was often involved in meetings the CEO of the company would attend, as well as the "C- level" officers of other Fortune 50 - 500 companies who were considered potential clients. These clients had flown in for these meetings from all over the world. There were some heavy hitters there.

In one of these meetings, there was a significant contingent of visiting officers in attendance. This company represented the potential for a very large amount of business. The CEO of the company I worked for at the time was very understated in his communication style. He didn't yell, scream or ever seem ruffled, just as you would expect from someone at that level. The image you have right now is probably correct. During this meeting, there was something the customer mentioned in passing. It wasn't a point of emphasis and was something most people wouldn't give a second thought to. Our CEO made the slightest eye contact with me for the briefest second. I knew what that meant. I immediately and quietly slipped out the back of the room because of that slight eye contact. Nobody noticed I had left.

It's HOW You Say It™

I knew that he had wanted me to follow up on the question the customer had. The phones sprang into action and in ten minutes there was a vice president I had contacted who dropped what he was doing and came to the room to personally shed more light on their question. That brief second of eye contact may have been what sealed a large opportunity because that attention to detail was conveyed, literally, in the blink of an eye (contact)!

People speak with their eyes whether or not they mean to. When you were a teenager and someone did something you thought was dumb, you made eye contact with your friends. Enough said. Communicating with your eyes is something that happens throughout your life -- sometimes, intentionally and with purpose, hoping for a specific outcome, and other times, unintentionally yet with impact.

In a business setting, the impact your eye contact has, or doesn't have, can communicate volumes about people's perceptions of you. I have the pleasure of mentoring several MBA and EMBA students from a local university graduate program. It's a wonderful experience, and I feel honored they have chosen me to participate as one of the mentors for the program. Most of these are adults who hold down full-time careers and are pursuing their advanced degrees during the evenings and weekends.

One of the participants is a gentleman who is an officer with a mid-sized company headquartered in the greater Kansas City area. He's been with the company a long time, has seen it go through some intense challenges, and has decided he'd like to look for an opportunity with a different company.

He mentioned he was used to interviewing others, but it had been a long time since he, himself, had been. He asked if I would give him some suggestions. The man is extremely intelligent and knows the business well.

We were meeting for lunch at a restaurant this particular day. I told him I'd be happy to help. I suggested we just chat for awhile and catch up on what was going on and that after we had eaten, we could switch to business, and I'd make a few suggestions. One of the behaviors I was looking for was his eye contact with me in different situations. I wanted to see the difference in how he communicated with me during conversations that he saw as relaxing and personal as opposed to work-related talk. Finally, how would he react when we started talking about the interviewing situation he had mentioned?

I noticed his comfort level and eye contact changed greatly depending upon what we happened to be talking about at the time. If we were talking about his running, something he loved to do and was good at, he looked right at me and his eyes seemed to light up. I could tell he loved the subject and was at ease talking about it.

After we ate, I changed the subject and said I was going to ask him a few questions that an interviewer might. This gentleman, although very intelligent, is also a quiet man. When I posed several of the questions he might be asked, I noticed that he seemed instantly less comfortable and didn't look directly at me. He would talk openly, but his eyes were across the room or focused on the soda he was holding. I mentioned this to him and told him the impact of this change: he seemed to lose his confidence, which in turn could make someone interviewing him question his experience, credibility and leadership capabilities. All because of his eyes.

In a later chapter, we'll talk about the challenges to communication, such as what my client faced, and how to correct those.

2. Your Voice

Your voice says so much about you. In the first seconds someone hears your voice for the first time, they make assumptions about you. Whether they can see you or not, perceptions are made about your physical appearance, your credibility, intelligence, patience, kindness and competence.

There are TV personalities, comedians, and actors who have built their careers around their distinctive voices. It evokes an impression of that person, whether valid or not. Just the sound of someone's voice can bring images to mind. When you hear the full, low tones of James Earl Jones, it automatically brings images of someone strong, in command and authoritative. I've asked someone too young to know who he is what they thought he looked like in person. They said big and muscular. I think he'd like to hear that!

I have one of those kinds of voices that is unmistakable. My voice is very low. When I first wake up in the morning, it's also raspy. It's not uncommon, if I have a cold, for someone to call on the phone, hear my voice, and ask if they have awakened me! At 1:30 in the afternoon, that's unlikely but my voice says differently.

Hearing someone's voice can bring different emotions, too. If you hear a parent's voice, your child's voice, a loved one or great friend, a manager, leader or political figure, all bring an instant emotional reaction and connection, or disconnect, to this specific communication. The tone and emotion in someone's voice when you hear, "Hello" often tells you exactly what kind of mood the speaker is in, just by the "temperature" of the voice.

When it comes to the office, your voice has a strong impact. It says much about the confidence you have, or lack thereof, the attitude you have towards others and even the amount of involvement you want to have. Many times a conversation can become disconnected because of the temperature of the other person's voice. What emotions do you feel they are contributing, disguising/withholding based on the warmth, or lack of the same? You can determine how involved a person wants to be based on this same temperature. There is an attitude that can be detected from the temperature in your voice. Does it seem to be "cool"? Does it give the impression to others that you aren't totally engaged, or does it have an "edge" to it?

When you receive a phone call from your manager, director or client, do you listen to hear what kind of temperature their voice has? You will have two responses to the temperature. You will either feel it "normal," possibly even a little "warm," causing you to feel open and receptive. Or it may sound "cool," causing you to feel a slight hesitation, curiosity or possibly a slight concern about the coming information.

One of the most popular keynote programs I do is, "It's Not Just What You Say, It's HOW You Say It." The voice is a big piece of that. In the workshop for this program, people can see themselves talk with others and hear the temperature of their voice in different scenarios. Although it may be unintentional, our voice changes with our comfort level. If you've ever worked with someone who you didn't feel a connection with, you may be surprised to hear the differences in the temperature of their voice, and yours, as you talk to different people in the room. The voice isn't the only factor that makes up this impression, but it's a good indicator of your listener's openness to what you are saying or contributing.

Especially in a leadership role, you will want to speak with confidence, empathy and conviction. That doesn't mean you need to speak loudly to be convincing. It means that the emotions you bring out in people should leave them with positive impressions of you. How you use your voice helps to build, or dampen, those emotions and their impact. Can you bring people to action simply by the temperature of your voice?

Your voice can elevate, or take away, your credibility. Do you know people who raise their voice at the end of a sentence when they talk? Reading that question just now may have you hearing the word "talk" go upward in inflection at the end. That wouldn't be unusual. Most people do raise their voice slightly at the end of the sentence when they ask a question. These people though, raise their voices in pitch at the end of every sentence. The last word goes up. Not only can that sound be very irritating, it also diminishes credibility as it makes the speakers appear uncertain you will believe what they are saying. It may give the impression they are trying to test the waters to see if you believe them. This is a trait that many people have and may not even be aware of. It's not a good habit to have and a difficult one to break.

We'll be talking in a later chapter about the reasons for disconnects in your communication. Your voice is one of these. There are easy steps you can take that, when practiced, will help your voice be your ally. We'll also talk about the challenges to communication and the steps you can take to improve them (The "It's HOW You Say It"™ Principle).

3. Posture, Body Language and Gestures

Let's just say it's hard for me, coming in at 6'0" tall, to sneak into a room. I can remember when I was younger, my mom used to say to me, "Stand up straight and be proud. Tall women are beautiful. Models are all tall." At the time, they all were. I thought it was just a ploy she used so that I wouldn't slouch. I really didn't think much of it until I saw a woman who was very tall, although much older than I was at the time, who didn't have good posture. My first impressions of her weren't very good. It hit me instantly what my Mom had been talking about.

There is a certain confidence, a certain elegance and stature, that you project when your posture is good. It really has nothing to do with your actual height and everything to do with how you carry yourself. While you don't want to appear rigid, you do want to make sure that your posture says, "Confidence." Just like your voice, you also want your posture to say, "I'm interesting." How do you do that?

Great posture is more than just standing up straight. If you are speaking in front of a group, how are you standing? Are you balanced equally on both feet, or are you standing with all your weight on one leg or the other? If so, all that credibility you've worked so hard for, is lost.

When you balance your weight all on one leg, it takes that "presence" I mentioned and throws it right down into the floor of the leg you are leaning on. Not good. Stand on your own two feet -- equally! Are your shoulders back? Not too rigid, or held to the point where you look unnatural, but push your shoulders back and hold your head up straight.

Let's talk a little more about your body language. Take the example of a conversation you're having at your office. Before you've spoken a word, the person/people you are talking with are making assumptions about you. Where are your arms? Are they crossed in front of you? That gives the impression you're closed to what's being discussed, even if you're just cold!

When you want to emphasize a point, or engage others in the conversation, there are several things you can do in a meeting:

With your body
- *Slightly* lean forward or rest your arms on the table in front of you.
- Use your hands to make small, general gestures. Watch how others use their gestures and try to make yours mirror those. Sincerity and being natural are always the best ways to go.
- Make sure your arms aren't crossed tightly in front of you. It gives the impression you are closed to their suggestions.
- Sit up tall

With your eyes
- Use the eye contact we talked about earlier. Engage those people at the meeting with your eyes to bring each person in. How? Look at each person and hold that look for 2-3 seconds. It's okay to scan the entire room although stopping and making direct eye contact will connect others to the conversation.
- Make sure to look directly at others when they are speaking.

With your voice
- Speak in an even and relaxed voice.
- Be conscious of your voice being sure not to elevate your voice at the end of your sentences.

- When on conference calls, stop periodically, and ask those on the phone what questions they have. Ask questions to those in the room also to keep them engaged, and ask the opinions of those on the phone from time to time for the same reason.

All of this will send signals to your listeners about your confidence, credibility, sincerity and interest in them and the topic.

How can you remember all this when you're presenting, or when you're participating in meetings? The following model can act as a job aid.

THE SPEAK MODEL

S.P.E.A.K.

In my presentations workshop, I go through an acronym I've created, S.P.E.A.K.
- *S*tand on your own two feet
- *P*rofessionalism, Passion, Presence
- *E*ngage
- *A*ction/Audience
- *K*eep it Real/Knowledge

Each letter of this acronym represents a strategy to follow and an action item for speaking in front of a live audience. The program is designed to help people who are delivering presentations get the support they need to have their audiences engage, not disengage.

If you aren't someone who will give presentations, is it still important? Absolutely. When your facial expressions and body language send a negative impression, it gives the people you are talking with that same impression of you: Negative. A presentation could be a meeting you're sharing your opinion in, or a meeting with a client or customer you're hoping to influence. While it may not seem important, your reputation in the workplace depends, in part, on the impressions you give. These impressions send a message that have an impact on perceptions: how committed you are to the goals of the organization and the projects that support them. If your words say one message, but your expressions and body language say another, it goes back to the old saying, "talk's cheap."

The Science of it All

The information I've shared in this book constitutes over 25 years of experience focused in and around the field of communication within corporate America. What you may not realize, is that while it made sense to me for over 25 years, it is backed up by science, as well!

Without trying to sound like Einstein, let's talk for a minute about neuroscience. What is that? Neuroscience is the study of the brain. What I've discovered, in essence, is that when you are happy and have a positive relationship, as in when you see someone you like or get along with come into the room, you release what's called oxytocins, a chemical in the brain. So if you've had a pleasurable experience with someone, like the person that brightens the room by walking into it, the next time you see them, you'll have an automatic happy feeling. Not just because of them coming in, rather because your body releases this chemical because it senses a positive, "safe" reaction to the person. It's similar to the relationship of a mother and child.

ALL ABOARD!

What messages are you communicating?

PART I   LAYING TRACKS

Let's talk about a few things you convey you may not know about. What does your posture say? Try this. Look at yourself in a mirror the way you usually stand. Stand sideways and look now. Are your shoulders back? Be conscious of standing straight and having good posture. It adds to your credibility and makes you appear confident.

What about your voice? What can you do?
- Speak in an even and relaxed voice.
- Be comfortable and familiar with what you're going to say, whether that's a presentation you're going to give, or just a topic you'll share information on at a meeting. It will make your voice less jittery and nervous.
- Record yourself. Most smart phones now have a recording application on them. If not, you can download several from your carrier's application store online. Listen to yourself. Do you think you are believable? Is the temperature of your voice warm? Do you sound scared, nervous or unsure? If it sounds that way to you, know that it will have twice that impact on others.
- Take a video! Smart phones allow you to take still pictures or videos. Turn it to video. While you're speaking, turn the camera toward your face and record for a minute or so. Play it back. Study your expression for the nonverbal messages you may be sending. Does the picture you see surprise you? Do you look happy or scared? Smile. It does wonders.

What messages are being sent?

Answer the questions by placing a checkmark in the appropriate box.

Situation	Activity	Yes	No
Meetings	•Look at the people participating in the meeting before it starts. Are they engaged in conversation with other participants?		
	• If engaged in conversation, are their bodies or faces turned towards each other when they speak?		
	• When someone speaks or makes a point during the meeting, does that person sit close to the table as opposed to having their chair farther back and away?		
	• Do any participants have their arms on the table or resting on notes as opposed to in their laps or folded across their bodies?		
	•When others speak, are participants making eye contact and paying attention to them?		
	• If a point is made that others disagree with, do they ask questions to gain understanding or do they take out their phones, look at the time, fold their arms and disengage?		

The more of the questions above that can be answered "yes," the better nonverbal messages are being sent about commitment to the meeting, its content and the people attending. What are your nonverbal messages conveying?

CHAPTER TWO

Communication Barriers

> *Words can build you up*
> *Words can break you down*
> *Start a fire in your heart or*
> *Put it out.*
> — Song lyrics from "Words" by Hawk Nelson

> *We judge others by their behavior.*
> *We judge ourselves by our intentions.*
> —Ian Percy - speaker

Barriers in communication between you and someone you work with begin before a word is spoken. While I was working with a client recently, she shared with me that although she's very knowledgeable in her field, there are times when she feels her message may not be received as she had hoped because she doesn't communicate as she'd like to in meetings. This is due, in part, to her lack of interpersonal communication skills. The challenge for her is the age-old "I don't know what I don't know." She said she was concerned more about how her message was going to be received than the content of what she was going to say.

When there's an idea you'd like to get across to a group of people, regardless of the size of the group, you need to consider this: What do you want the group to do when you are finished? Determine this yourself before you ever go into the meeting. If you don't know the answer to this, neither will they.

So you have a great strategy to move forward, right? Not necessarily. Let's take a look at some of the most common challenges to communication.

In this chapter, we'll also look at perceptions of those you work with and around, even though you may not be aware these perceptions exist. These barriers can also be wedges in communicating with friends and family.

Let's take a look at the seven challenges to effective communication:

1. Our History Together
2. Appearances
3. Different Personalities
4. "He and She"
5. Agendas in the Workplace
6. Your Reputation
7. Do I Care?

1. Our History Together

Many times, especially within a small company, or the same department of a larger company, it's common to have certain people you work with daily, and some who you work on specific projects with. It may be this person has a similar skill set, or just the opposite, and you are thrown together because of the diverse talents you both/all bring to the table. That's not a bad thing, unless the relationship and history makes you dread seeing that person before they're even there.

PART I LAYING TRACKS

You've heard the saying that some people brighten a room just by walking into it. The opposite is also true. Some people really brighten a room by walking OUT of it! You may feel that way about someone in your work group. Even worse, someone may feel that way about you. While it's not uncommon to like some people more than others, when your history with a person impacts a project, meeting, or the environment people work in day-to-day, it's time to re-evaluate.

Imagine that you have a communication "teeter-totter." When you first meet someone, the teeter-totter is balanced; you haven't formed an opinion of the person yet. You may have an "influencer," someone who has told you something about the person you've just met, or who's had exposure to a project the new person has been on, or possibly an interaction they've had with the same person. For the most part though, that relationship is still at a balance.

Imagine that every time you communicate with them, and they with you, it affects that balance. If the conversation is positive, and how they communicate with you leaves you with a good, positive feeling, then trust with that person is slowly starting to build, as is the relationship.

If that's the case, the communication leans ever-so-slightly to the positive side. If the interaction seems slightly "off," they have a cool temperature to their tone of voice, they aren't really engaged and listening to you, the balance leans ever-so-slightly to the negative side. After a while, there will be more of one than another, and your impression and opinion of that person will start to lean either to the positive, or the negative side, respectively. After several interactions with this person, you form an opinion. Whether positive or negative at this point, it takes quite a few interactions of the opposite kind to start to move that impression the other way.

When you have had a less than great experience with someone in your work group or on your project team, do you react to them in a different way than others? You may tend to discount their suggestions because they're the one saying it. Do you just ignore them altogether?

When there is history with a person at work, it can be due to several factors: They may have spoken badly about you behind your back and you've found out. They may act with an air of superiority, as if theirs are the only ideas that are good or the only opinions that matter. It may be the temperature of their voice. You may interpret the tone of their voice as disrespectful or slightly condescending or cold.

They may have challenged your ideas, possibly publicly in meetings, or unprofessionally. They might have challenged or assaulted your character or treated you poorly or have acted insensitively toward you. They might have taken credit for ideas that were yours, damaged your credibility or even lied to you. It may be they have broken a trust or acted without integrity or, possibly, without ethics.

Joe Calhoon, resepcted speaker and author of "The 1-Hour Plan to Growth," shared something with me that hit home and bears repeating. He said, "If someone says something about you that is true, you have no right to be upset. If they say something that's not true, you have no reason." Words of wisdom.

This says nothing about a history with someone at the office who you have had a social friendship or personal relationship with that has deteriorated, and now you're faced with bringing those repercussions into the work environment. In this situation, the true question you have to judge is "Do I really care if this relationship works?" Until you can answer this question by saying it IS important to you, nothing else will change the situation.

Regardless of how much you do or don't like the person you have a history with, remember to treat them with honesty and integrity. That way if they try to say something bad about your character, they can't! They may not like you, but they know your word is your word and that your actions are always above board.

With that said, building a foundation of trust is paramount in good communication. Why, you ask? You don't need to trust to talk. However, if that person feels they can trust you, they will perceive your communications, and your intentions, as positive. If they don't trust you, they second guess your motives and are hesitant to readily agree with your ideas. Their trust of you, and their perceptions of your integrity will have an impact on their willingness to accept the messages you communicate in a positive light.

I asked 200 people at a conference in Kansas City to assemble into groups to talk about projects they've worked on and the traits of those on the team that drove them nuts and caused issues within the team. Although there were many different groups discussing this, two common themes occurred. First, people who tried to act like they knew everything and tried to dominate the group and the conversation were huge challenges. They said those same people, if they feel they aren't getting their way, will disrupt the group and try to get others in side conversations to agree with them. That way, they can then push ahead with the "safety in numbers" approach. The second resounding theme was those who didn't listen to others. It sounds as though they are on the same approach as the above group; it appeared theirs was the only worthy conversation. When you, or anyone else spoke, it seemed they were already formulating what to come back with. When this happens, trust deteriorates and walls are built. These histories can overshadow meetings, projects or conversations.

2. Appearances

You've heard the men's hygiene commercial that says you don't get a second chance to make a first impression. How true! The second challenge to communication is the effect your appearance has on the person/people you are interacting with. Should I stay or should I go? Your appearance is, obviously, not a verbal communication but it "speaks" volumes about you nonetheless and is a critical factor in "It's HOW You Say It."™ Your appearance, or someone's "impression" of you based on your appearance, may be unintentional, but it's extremely hard to change once made. Many assumptions are made about your appearance that can filter your impressions of another's intelligence, income, personality and even grooming habits.

Know that two different people may interpret your appearance differently based on corporate culture, their gender, age group or personal preference. If I'm looking for a creative advertising agency, when I walk in the door and see people wearing jeans, long hair, gauges in their ears and sandals on their feet, I may think, "Wow, they go against the status quo and I want an agency that's creative and not afraid to go against convention!" On the other hand, if I'm going into a bank, and it's important to me to feel that my money is secure, and there's a feeling of maturity and an established approach of convention present, I want the employees to present themselves professionally and dress conservatively, my impression of what makes this bank a place in which I want to do business. "Hmm, they don't look like they take risks with what they wear. I'm thinking they won't take an uncalculated, wild risk with my finances either." I want them to dress the same way I want them to handle my money. What's appropriate in one situation may be totally inappropriate in another. What to do?

While the jury disagrees on the length of time it takes to make a first impression about someone's appearance, here are two I found in my research that surfaced numerous times.

According to a University of Toledo psychology professor, Dr. Frank Bernieri, first impressions are formed within 30 seconds. However, from a December, 2002 article published in *USA Today*:

> **It takes only three to five seconds to make a first impression, but it can take a whole career to undo it.**
> —Dana May Casperson, author of *Power Etiquette: What You Don't Know Can Kill Your Career.*

Most people in a business environment are conscious that being neat and clean is expected. While you may think presenting yourself with a professional appearance requires money, it is not necessarily so. There are many ways of giving a positive first impression that cost next to nothing but make a strong impact. I am forever amazed at the lack of concern some have for the image they project. I have seen people, both new and tenured, who come to work with their clothes, especially shirts, unironed, and their hair a mess. They appear as though they tumbled out of bed and into the office. If you give the impression you don't care about yourself, you're also

It's HOW You Say It™

giving the impression you don't care about your career. If it doesn't appear that you have respect for yourself, it can effect the level of respect others have for you and show to you. You are sabotaging yourself needlessly.

How well people are accepted because of their appearance also varies depending upon the culture of the company or business they are in. For instance, if you work for an entrepreneurial start-up in a technology field, it may be totally acceptable to come to work in jeans and sporting a piercing, with your hair in dreadlocks or highlighted in a bright fuchsia. It may fit into a culture of creativity and imagination. It could also give clients the impression you are just the perfect person to come up with that out-of-the-box idea they've been looking for. However, if you are a leader in the finance industry, wanting to give clients the appearance of stability, maturity, experience and professionalism, coming in dressed as the example above may have your customers heading for the door.

How you are groomed -- nails, hair, clothes, hygiene -- is only a part of the effect your physical appearance can have. Remember the posture we talked about in Chapter One? You guessed it: that has an impact as well. You are communicating much about yourself through your dress, whether you mean to or not. When it comes to communication, your clothes and grooming are another example of "HOW You Say It" -- in this case, "speaking" volumes about you.

Over-dressing may be as dangerous to "HOW You Say It" as dressing down. You may give the wrong impression by wearing a suit and not realize it. How you wear your clothes sends messages. For instance, let's say you work in an environment where the company dress code says jeans are acceptable each day. In your position, you don't interact directly with external customers and have no responsibilities that would suggest a different dress than other employees in your same position. If you wear a suit to work, for no apparent reason, it may give the impression you're arrogant, or feel you are in some way better or superior to the others in your same position, or that you will be attending a funeral later in the day! It may suggest you're trying to "impress the boss" by associating yourself in ways bosses dress. If you're wearing that suit, and it doesn't fit well or it's not tailored properly, it can also give the opposite impression, that you don't fit the image of someone whose position suggests that dress, because you aren't able to wear the look professionally now.

Recently, I was talking with a manager in a leading, national cable company. It's a wonderful company and the executive leadership should be the envy of other companies. This woman was bright, knew the business and the industry itself well and had great organizational skills. While this all sounds good, her challenge was this: She was very petite, had long, blond hair and was physically very fit. She wore suits with skirts and accented them with high, platform heels. Both are in style. The challenge was, at times, the skirts on the suits were a touch too short. There were also times when the blouses she wore were slightly low cut or slightly too tight. Because of that, combined with her blond hair and effervescent personality, she could have been being perceived as "flighty" and people may not have been taking her seriously. Her shoes were very stylish, although the heels were too high for a business environment. I suggested she get a more conservative, professional business look that would project the image of the leadership level she wanted to achieve.

Appearances can be deceiving. Once you've made that first impression, whatever it is, it will take much more time to change an impression than to make one.

3. Different Personalities

This pretty much says it all. People are different. While many people say when it comes to love, opposites attract, in business, it may be the opposite.

Take this example. Let's say there's a meeting. There are two types of people that will be coming to that meeting. Mickie, gets there 10 - 15 minutes early. She has her pen, her notepad, tablet or laptop and her cup of coffee. She's sitting at the table ready to go.

Elaina, gets there at about five minutes till. She comes flying in the door, talking as she comes, "Oh my gosh, did you see the traffic on 435? I thought I'd never get here. Wow, I need coffee. Do you need coffee? Be right back, ya, coffee."

Mickie is thinking, "I wish she would sit down and shut up." Elaina is thinking, "Wow, she needs to chill out and get a life." Neither one is wrong as long as the meeting starts on time. They are just different.

What happens, though, is they have set up this "Us and Them" silent army attitude; yet a word to each other may not have been spoken yet. How does this look? "Us" doesn't sit next to "Them" in meetings or at functions. When someone new comes into the room, you look to see if they sit with "Us" or if they sit with "Them." During projects or meetings, you may listen to "Them," but their ideas could never be as good as one that comes from "Us." A wedge begins to push into the group, and you may not even have a solid idea of why!

Many factors can cause this "us and them" mentality to flourish. People want to have a feeling of belonging. Just like back in high school, you love to feel like you're part of a group, wether it be cheerleaders and basketball players, or delinquents and misfits.

In corporate America, we want to feel like we belong, too. That may be "Us" the laborers against "Them" the management. It may be "Us" with an American heritage and background against "Them," the Asian/Hispanic/Muslim or other culture different from our own. This is due, in large part, because we don't feel we are being understood or our viewpoint is being heard or appreciated.

> *A riot is the language of the unheard.*
> —Martin Luther King, Jr.

4. "He and She"

To say that men and women communicate differently is the understatement of several centuries. While the previous three reasons for challenges to communication are important (Our History Together, Appearances, Different Personalities), this one can be difficult because we don't really realize it's happening until it's made an impact, and even then sometimes we're not sure what hit us.

The author of *GenderTalk Works: Seven Steps for Cracking the Gender Code,* Connie Glaser, says, "The problem between men and women in the workplace is not the fact that they play by a different set of rules. The problem is they don't know the rules." Take, for example, her story about a scene she observed in the headquarters of a large corporation. A group of high-level women was standing in the hall as a man approached. The women opened the circle, inviting the man to join the conversation. Men, however, would not have made that effort.

"Including is just not part of the male culture. Men don't ask to be included. If they want in, they jump in," said Glaser. Women, may hesitate and wait to be invited. If the invitation doesn't present itself, they may feel unaccepted or unwelcome.

Communication Trait	Women	Men
Body Language	• Body alignment, face the other person • Use more hand gestures • Use more bodily contact • Sat relatively still	• Desire space • Tend to be withdrawn rather than engaged bodily • Do not touch, unless with same gender in playful aggression • Tend to move around and shift body when conversation is uncomfortable
Facial Expression	• Use eye-to-eye contact • Use less head motion than men • Tend to express emotion through facial expression • Smile more	• Don't use a lot of eye contact • Use more head motion • Conceal and control facial displays • Smile less
Speech	• Use conversation to negotiate closeness and intimacy • Talking is the essence of intimacy; sitting and talking means friendship • Speaking about problems is the essence of connection • Rule by consensus; get the input of others to make a decision • Go in-depth on a topic	• Use talk to assert their independence • Sitting and talking is not an essential part of friendship • Hear talk of problems as a request for advice or help • Give orders as a way of gaining social status • Use more small talk

I've noticed in corporate environments, that when it comes to meetings where important decisions will be made, women tend to "get their ducks in a row," and make sure they are ready. Men, tend to chat about the upcoming meeting "around the water cooler." Men may ask what the other thinks and how they may vote for the decision to be made. For men, often, the meeting itself is a formality. They know what's going to be brought up and how the vote will go. Women come to the meeting expecting a meeting, often to find out it seems the real meeting was held without them and discussion and decisions were made before-hand. Although not intentionally to exclude them, it happens none-the-less.

The style of communication between men and women can also be different. Women tend to come across as less self-confident than men. For example, many women start a phrase by discounting themselves before they've said anything: "You've probably already thought about this, but... ." They may also start a conversation with an apology: "I'm sorry, this... ." Because of the approach, they are giving the signal they aren't as knowledgeable, confident or aware as others in the room. They may also seek approval as though they aren't confident in their own suggestion to stand on its own merit: "Don't you agree?" "Or not?"

Some of the most common differences in communication between men and women were identified by Dr. John Gray.

Online communication within the genders varies as much as it does face to face, according to the experts. Researcher Susan C. Herring conducted a study on male/female email communications at Indiana University. There was an apparent difference in the language used by males and females online. Aggressive expressions used in emails by males far outnumbered those used by females--12 to 5. In online communication, whether it be through email, instant message or in a forum, men tended to be authoritative and gain valuable information, while women tended to nurture existing relationships and develop new ones.

5. Agendas in the Workplace

Although not as easily perceived, one of the challenges to effective communication in the workplace is the agenda that may be at work behind the scenes. These may be subtle, but personal agendas can sabotage the relationship and, therefore, the communication.

How do you know if someone is working from their own agenda? It may look something like this: You have an idea, that all of a sudden has turned into "their" idea. It may be just a piece of the idea, but it's an important piece. It may be these people won't share information, the mentality being they work on the premise of "knowledge is power." This may make them feel they are able to exert an advantage over anyone who doesn't have the information they do. They may tend to over exaggerate the impact of an idea they have. When pushed for detail or numbers, the blame will be pointed to anyone but themselves, hoping to stay in the "favored" light.

Take heart. People that have a hidden agenda, usually don't target just one person, unless you're their biggest competition. Although that may not be a comfort, people around you, leadership included, will catch on to this. You don't need to bring it to light because everyone already sees it.

6. Your Reputation

Fair or not, your reputation precedes you. People want to work for, and be associated with success. If you have a great reputation, you're perceived to be successful and people will treat you with a certain amount of respect and kindness. If you know or are one of these people, you have most certainly earned this status because you have demonstrated professionalism, ethical behavior, and positive attitude. You are encouraging and accepting of others. A lot of this goes back to the "History" we talked about earlier.

If someone coming to the team has had a bad experience with another team member, it's not unusual for one to put that person in a "less than perfect light." Many times, this is an insecurity. "Do unto others before they do unto you," or so it seems. If they have an insecurity about that relationship, or how it will be the next time based on the history, it's possible they will make sure everyone on a new project would be on their "side" should there be a clash.

Know that this goes both ways. Although it's hard not to respond, the best thing you can do is nothing. Just like a fire without wood goes out, if you don't add to "the fire," the gossip will die out.

7. Do I Care?

It could truly all come down to this.

People have different reasons for wanting to make things work. It may be a personal relationship you have that's important to you. It may be a business relationship that's important to you, or it may be that it's in your best interest to make it succeed. However, if you look at a situation, or at the person/people who are involved, and you can say to yourself, "I really don't care what happens," that's the end of the discussion. If your heart isn't in it, your efforts won't be either.

In the end, either nothing will change, or you'll make matters worse by your lack of sincerity.

If you truly do want to improve your relationships, be a better manager, a better leader and a value-driven person, read on. If you have the will to succeed, you're already on the right track. Don't be overwhelmed. It's one step at a time.

When I was a little girl, my mom used to read me stories from a set of blue story books. The pages were illustrated and I would lean against her as she read to me. One of my favorites... The *Little Engine That Could* by Watty Piper.

You are now leaving the station. Your mantra, "I think I can, I think I can." Just keep chugging.

What the "It's HOW You Say It"™ principle can't do, is step number one in my program, "The Personalities of Conflict - Which One Are YOU?" That first step is to judge whether you really do want to improve the relationship or the situation. If you don't have a desire to make it work, and you aren't sincere in the steps you take, it's all a moot point.

The Science of It All

David Rock *Your Brain at Work* said that your memories of your social interconnections are vast. Elephants aren't the only ones who will never forget when it comes to harboring a long memory if we've been wronged by someone, or FEEL we've been wronged.

As mentioned in "The 6 Reasons for Disconnect," from our earlier chapter, if you have a negative history of experiences with someone, whatever the reason is, I believe you're also more likely to focus on the other person themselves during a meeting than the actual content and objectives of the meeting itself.

For instance, if that person is at a meeting that you're involved in too, you may be wondering if they are going to have a hidden agenda, are thinking about how much they don't like you, or generally may think about trying to sabotage you. When they speak, you're on high alert.

Robert B. Cialdini, author of, *Harnessing the (Behavioral) Science of Persuasion*, says there are 6 Principles of Persuasion:

1) The Principle of Liking: People Like Those Who Like Them
2) The Principle of Reciprocity: People Repay in Kind
3) The Principle of Social Proof: People Follow the Lead of Similar Others
4) The Principle of Consistency: People Align with Their Clear Commitments
5) The Principle of Authority: People Defer to Experts
6) The Principle of Scarcity: People Want More Of What They Can Have Less Of

The Seven Challenges to Communication discussed in this chapter are supported by the science of Cialdini's research. If you look at them together, his research supports what I have shared in the content of this chapter.

All Aboard

"HOW to Say It." Share your information in a format and flow that are easy for the listeners to follow. For instance, remind them of the status quo, and how things are now. What is it that's not being accomplished because of the current state, and why is there a need for change? Present your suggestion of what you believe should change, or the action you'd like them to take. Let them know the possible positive results that can happen for the revenue, the business, the customer, or other business demands from taking the action or suggestion you're presenting. Be specific. Share a high-level overview of how you are envisioning the change taking place: How do you see this change being implemented? Summarize by reiterating the need for the change and your confidence in the outcomes you're suggesting. Know that what you are suggesting IS in the best interest of your customer, and convey that!

As you prepare to do the suggestion above, keep in mind the challenges to communication mentioned in this chapter. Present your idea in a way that will neutralize those challenges before they happen. Be mindful of how they see the seven challenges to communication, as it relates to their experiences with you.

PART II

AVOIDING TRAIN WRECKS AND STAYING ON TRACK

Part II couples in Chapters III and IV to give you information, science and skills for your wild ride through management.

You have the train heading in the right direction and you're picking up steam. You understand where your journey has taken you so far and are building the foundational skills to ensure you can switch directions when needed.

The challenge now will be keeping a watchful eye to ensure you're not heading for the train wrecks that often happen in communication. These can derail the best of relationships and keep new ones from developing along a positive route. Although your messages may be well-intentioned, let's take a look at the reasons the best of intentions can crash and how to get back on the right track.

All Aboard

CHAPTER THREE
The Five "Disconnects"

In Chapter Two we talked about the seven challenges you face in your conversations before a word has been spoken: History, Appearance, Personalities, Gender, Agendas, Reputation and Do I Care. There are ways that you communicate and send messages through the words you use. It's not just what you say, "It's HOW You Say It."™

Have you been in a situation where someone said something to you, and it just didn't sit right? Only to have someone else say, "Oh, I think you took that the wrong way. I don't think they meant it like that." Don't you wonder, why they took it the "right" way, yet you took it the "wrong" way? Some of this goes back to the trust and history that we talked about in the previous chapter.

Very often though, these are examples of how we've said something, or how someone else has said something, that's caused the impact of the worded message to break down.

In Chapter Three, "It's HOW You Say It,"™ we'll take a look at five reasons HOW you say something may be the reason what you say isn't being received the way you intended.

1. Your Approach
2. Nonverbals
3. Tone of Voice

4. Reaction/Response
5. You're Thinking Like You

1. Your Approach

Many times the reason our communication doesn't sit right with the person we are trying to get a message to is because of our approach.

Let me illustrate. I love my husband dearly. He covers an NFL team for a national sports network. He's used to deadlines, facts, figures and prima donnas. When he's busy, he can become extremely direct. For example, I may call to him upstairs and say, "Do you want to leave at 7:00?" His response may be, "Give me 13 seconds. I'm right in the middle of this. I promise you I'll be with you in 13 seconds." He didn't say, "I need a minute." Being extremely precise can be interpreted as being too direct. He didn't literally mean 13 seconds, what he meant was I'm not ready and I'm feeling pressured.

In my mind, it took him twice as long to go into the reason he couldn't talk than it would have for him to give me a simple "7:30's better," or, "I need a few minutes." Either of those responses are less precise. Therefore, I would have perceived them as being less direct. His approach to my question was frustrating. Although I know and love him, if he were to respond to someone who didn't know him with that direct approach, it could negatively impact their perception of him.

Sometimes, someone's approach may not elicit frustration, it may be perceived as being mean or rude. Take this example: Let's say you are a sales representative. Your manager has asked you to come to the office that morning to go over some sales figures. Before you get there, he/she has received a phone call and they're on a deadline to put out "a fire." They have an hour to get something to the VP and it will take a lot of time.

PART II   AVOIDING TRAIN WRECKS AND STAYING ON TRACK

Let's see the difference it makes to the sales rep based on two different ways the manager could approach this. The differences, and how the message is received, are solely due to the manager's approach. The difference is clear -- "It's HOW You Say It."™

Scenario A

"Oh, hi [huffy breath]. As usual, I've gotten a phone call that's changed my whole day. I'm not going to be able to spend any time with you, but I have to give you these numbers anyway. Wow, I'm dying of thirst. I don't have time to get this done for Jim and I really don't have time to talk to you. You know what, run down the hall, get me a glass of water and when you come back, we'll have to go through the numbers, or I'll hear it for that, too. Don't stop to talk to anyone because I'm out of time today. That's just the way it is."

Because the manager has position power, the rep may get the glass of water. I wouldn't drink it if you know what I mean! All the way down the hall, however, the rep is probably thinking, "The manager asked me to come in. Get water--go fetch your own water!"

This interaction has put a stress on that relationship. This experience will now be part of the sales representative's "history" with this manager. The next time they get together, he/she will be thinking about the treatment they received this last time they met--go fetch their water!

Let's take the same situation with a different approach. When the rep comes in this time...

Scenario B

"Hi. How's it going? Make it through the construction okay? Hey, thanks for coming in. I got a phone call right before you came. Jim needs some information from me that, unfortunately, is going to take some time to put together. I want to be considerate of your time, too. Would it be okay with you if we cut our time short? I do want to go over the numbers, that's important, I just can't take much time today. Wow, I'm so thirsty. Hey, could I ask you a big favor? Do you mind going to the break room and getting a glass of water for me? I'd really appreciate it. While you're gone, I'll pull the reports and when you get back we can look at those, I'll answer any questions you may have, and let's schedule a follow up for the end of the week to go over any concerns you have that we won't get to today. Does that work for you?"

In both examples, all the manager's objectives are met. They go over the sales figures, and the manager gets a drink of water. The difference is, because of the approach the second time, the manager hasn't left the rep angry and frustrated. They've preserved the relationship, in part, because of the approach.

Let's take a look at various approaches in the way people communicate, why they don't work, and how their styles are perceived by others.
- The Controller
- The Pleaser
- The Reproacher

The Controller

You may know people in leadership positions who have a very direct and harsh approach: "My way or the highway." They use their position power to "strongarm you" into doing what they want. These people can be controlling and dominating. It is a battle each time you meet. They are seldom open to other's thoughts or suggestions and tend to feel their way is always the right way. This approach can ruin relationships and cause hard feelings these leaders may never be aware of. The same could be true of you. Think about how your approach may look to someone else.

The Pleaser

The opposite can also be frustrating from an effective communication standpoint. What about those people who are gelatin? You ask them something and their response is to apologize, be indecisive, withhold opinion, avoid saying what they're afraid may be the wrong thing. Their approach may be to say whatever "the boss" says. These situations are true, and frustrating, both in the business world and personal life.

Early in our lives we may have learned the lesson that we're expected to always have the right answers, to always be right. As adults, if we're concerned we may not be, we tend to defer to the person/people we feel have the answers, or at least the answer people are expecting. In order to appear correct, we ask for their opinions or suggestions and then agree with them. Each approach can be frustrating to those in the work group or to the family at home. If you're going to make a decision, right or wrong, gather your facts, weigh the probable outcomes and decide with conviction even if you're wrong. If you never make a mistake, there's not an opportunity to learn.

The Reproacher

Some people's approach is often a "reproach." No matter what you do, it's not good enough, fast enough, detailed enough, or general enough. You get the idea. They love to change something just for the sake of having their name on it, too. Their approach is to eat away at your self-confidence to make themselves feel more important.

2. Nonverbals

It's not only the approach that people use, there are also many nonverbals that are processed and taken into consideration.

> *Dr. Wilson: What exactly did Cuddy tell you?*
> *Dr. House: Nothing that your body language isn't telling me right now.*
> —The televised drama "House"

How true! What messages are you sending? How are you standing? Are you facing directly or at an angle, as if you're looking for a quick escape? Are your arms crossed in front of you as if nothing they say can make you "open"? Do you/they look bored just being around? Is their focus on everything else in the room except you? If you're in their office, are they preoccupied and looking at emails, texts or searching for things on their desks?

At the beginning of Chapter Three, the first reason for disconnect in "How You Say It," is your approach. Part of that approach (Reason number 2) can be the nonverbal messages you are sending... or receiving!

Let's assume you are one-on-one with someone having a conversation. Do they have eye contact with you? If so, do their eyes look bright and interested, or narrowed and agitated? There are many factors that go into our perception of how we interpret the conversations we have. Many of these interpretations are also based upon experiences with these people as mentioned in the previous chapter.

Do you normally get along well with them? If so, you're more likely to let it slide if they seem a little uninterested, or their body language says they don't have time for you right then. If, on the other hand, this person is someone you brace for every time you know you will meet, you're more likely to have your guard up and look for signs in their body language that you can take negatively, just to reinforce your ongoing thought that you two don't get along, and they're the reason!

Let's take this scenario. Let's say you are having a meeting with your team. "Mary" is someone who has a history of always pushing back when something new is introduced, or so it seems to you. It's frustrating and you know that no matter what the subject of the meeting is, there will be something that she won't like. During the meeting, you're introducing a new administrative practice. You know she's going to be negative and not support this at all and you are almost dreading this meeting. Sure enough, you share what's going on, and Mary's the first to huff. She may even sit back in her seat and disengage from the rest of the conversation. Before you blame it all on Mary, think about this. What were your body language and your nonverbals saying? Were you avoiding eye contact with her, hoping she wouldn't say anything if you didn't look at her. Was your body language "including" her or were you facing away?

> *It doesn't matter what you have to say, it matters what they see when you say it.*
> — Speaker Patricia Fripp, CSP, CPAE

Another subtle, or not so subtle, nonverbal is the brief eye contact with someone else. Remember when you were in high school? If someone, who wasn't "in" said something, for just the briefest moment, you'd look at your friend across the table or next to you and make that eye contact. Did Mary do that during the meeting? Although no words were spoken, everyone else in the room knew the message she was sending. Some things never change!

Another example of nonverbals that have an impact are your eyes themselves. What is the temperature of that nonverbal? Is it warm, inviting and accepting, or cold, disinterested and judgmental? Do your eyes engage while someone is talking, or are you looking around the room because you're uncomfortable having extended eye contact? If so, and you tend to look away, you send the message that you lack confidence, or you don't really feel their conversation is important. If you're leading the conversation, it can send the message you aren't sure you know what you're talking about.

3. Tone of Voice

This, to me, holds the most impact. The tone in someone's voice may sound as though they want to make you feel welcome and invited. The "temperature" of their voice is also an integral part of tone and together make up the third example of why "It's HOW You Say It" ™ is so crucial.

Let me explain the difference in the two. The tone in someone's voice refers to how they are saying their words. Do they sound as though they want you there and are glad to see you? The temperature, however, is the underlying emotions of their tone. For instance, they may say they're glad you're there, and the sound, or tone, may support that but what emotion does it bring out in you? Do you truly believe they mean that, or is there that certain "something" that makes you feel it's insincere and just "talk?" The temperature of their voice is the emotion you read behind the words and surface sound of the words they use. Does the temperature prompt you to feel kindness and acceptance from them or exclusion and indifference under the surface of what they say? Is the tone of their voice and the temperature the same, or is there a distinct difference you detect?

In 2010 Sandy (Alex) Pentalnd, director of Massachusetts Institutes of Technology's Human Dynamics Lab, was challenged with a study. Could it be predicted? The challenge: Can we really tell who will succeed in competitive business situations without knowing what they have to offer?

Pentland explains, "This study not only confirms previous research—we've used data on social signals to predict the outcome of salary negotiations and even who would 'survive' a plane crash in a NASA role-playing game—but takes it further. This time we collected the data well before the event whose outcome we predicted. But in all the situations, these social cues—what we call 'honest signals'—were powerful indicators of success."

> *The finding: "It's not what you say, it's how you say it..."*

Tone of voice can change the impression and perception of your messages, whether or not you're aware of it. If someone shares an idea with you, you may respond by saying, "That's interesting." Your tone of voice though, may actually be conveying the message, "That's the dumbest thing I've ever heard." The temperature of your voice may say, "I'm so bored I can't stand it."

One of the best examples of this was unintentionally given to me by my then 14-year-old daughter. I had been at a meeting earlier in the day. The meeting ended around noon and the people there asked if I'd join them for lunch. I told them I thought that sounded great. They asked me what kind of food I liked. "I like pretty much anything. I'm easy going when it comes to lunch, so whatever." We chose Thai food. It was good and we had a great time.

When I got home later that afternoon, our daughter was enjoying the benefits of summer vacation. When I walked in the door, she was sprawled across the couch. She had one leg flung over the back of the couch, the other stretched down onto the floor, and she was lying on her back, listening to her iPod and texting on her phone as if lightning had struck her. "Hi!" I said. "Hhmm," I think was the reply.

I happened to look into the kitchen. There were dirty dishes everywhere. One of her chores is to clear the table, load and unload the dishwasher and clean the counters. A torture she has assured us we are the only parents in the world who inflict. In looking around, I could tell none of this had happened.

I calmly walked over to the couch and said, "Honey, I need you to put down your phone for awhile and clean the kitchen. If we leave those dirty dishes out, we'll get ants. Once we have them, we can't get rid of them."

She clunked her one foot to the floor, dragged her leg down from the back of the couch, flung it onto the floor and very slowly stood up -- all 5'10" of her. She rolled her eyes slightly, gave me one of those "huffy breaths," looked me in the eyes and said, "WhatE-V-E-R."

"WhatE-V-E-R?" I took a deep breath, walked up to her, leaned in and looked HER right in the eyes and uttered those words every teenager is loathe to hear, "Your phone is MINE!"

"But, Mom, whatever isn't a bad word! This is so unfair! You'd be shocked to hear what other kids at my school say!"

Well, she'd be shocked to hear that those words weren't created when she was a freshman in high school. "Mom, you always tell me not to over react to things, to take a deep breath and think about it for a minute." She's right, I have said that. So, I stopped, took a deep breath and thought about it. PHONE GONE!

The reason I have shared her story is this: The word that got her precious phone taken away, is the same word I had used just hours before to share what I wanted to eat for lunch, "whatever."

We all use the same words. No matter who we talk to or what we talk about, all of us have the same choice of words with which to communicate. It's not what she said, it was how she said it.

In a business environment, it has the same impact. Because we're all trying to be very "PC," we aren't as obvious as a teenager when it comes to the tone of voice. Even when extremely subtle, the feeling comes across. The temperature of your message may not even be conveying attitude. Just the opposite, you may be conveying, "I just could not care less."

Conducted by some of the most prestigious institutions in the country, studies were done to determine if the tone of voice a surgeon used had any impact on whether or not they were involved in malpractice cases.

Does tone of voice have a subconscious impact? Yes.

From the Department of Psychology, Harvard University, Boston, MA; Department of Psychology, University of California-Riverside, Riverside, CA; Legacy Good Samaritan

Hospital, Portland, OR; and University of Toronto, Toronto, Ontario, Canada - Conclusions: Surgeons' tone of voice in routine visits is associated with malpractice claims history. This is one study that shows clear associations between communication and malpractice in surgeons.

So, are you thinking you can't do anything right? Don't despair, in the next chapter we'll talk about The Six-Step, "It's HOW You Say It"™ Principle.

4. Reaction/Response

In addition to your approach, your nonverbals and your tone of voice, how you react to someone, the way you say it, has a great impact on how they perceive you. This can also impact the impressions they form of you and their willingness to try, or want, to make a relationship work.

Although we've taken individual components, like non-verbals and tone of voice, the combined impact to communication when you react inappropriately, especially in a business situation, can have project-wide implications.

There are five common ways reactions or responses negatively impact a relationship either in business or in personal situations. If you demonstrate one or more of these reactions or responses, here's how others may be perceiving and interpreting your communication:

A. The Winner

Dave reacts as though he's in the Superbowl. He needs to win at ALL costs. He is always right, in his own mind, no matter what. This doesn't mean he conveys that by raising his voice, although he might. He gives, through his responses and reactions, nonverbals and emphasis, as well as intonation and eye movement, the impression that if you disagree with him, you're obviously <u>wrong</u>!

Should you push back or disagree, he is the first to start a side conversation to get those around him to rally behind him. If it is a two-person conversation, he may demean you, pull rank or name drop someone of importance who agrees with him. The way he says it may be subtle, especially in a business situation. But it will happen if you don't see and agree with the direction he is trying to push.

This disruptive behavior is a power play, sometimes by those in management or leadership positions, and sometimes by team members. The key in any of the roles mentioned above is they are very competitive and, in the quest to be right, tend to be rather controlling.

B. Add My Two Cents

Natalie needs to feel as though she has knowledge, and is well informed, of absolutely anything that's being discussed. She also wants people to think she is intelligent, and "How You Say It," for her, is to have an answer for just about any question that is asked to anyone!

If you work with a person like this, you may think they're full of hot air. They may be! Just like a balloon is full of "hot air," sometimes we need to step back, let them "squeak" a little, or let their words "fly around the room" for a time so they can get that air out. Once that balloon, their need to talk, has been expended, you can talk with them more realistically. Like the child in grade school who wants to answer the question so badly they are almost standing up in their chair to raise that hand higher to be heard, so is the person who wants to add their two cents to the conversation.

They may have, even unintentionally, a very slight arrogance to their voice when they add a comment, or they may not. You can ask them anything and they know the answer.

c. The Screamer

If you react like "The Screamer," you communicate several messages with "How You Say It".™ One screamer may resemble Bobby Knight. Bobby Knight used to be a college basketball coach known for his volatile temper. Some people think he used to intentionally scream at officials during a game just to motivate and stir up his players. Effective? What he was teaching those young men was that it was okay, and acceptable, to scream at other people to get what he wanted.

In business, you see some managers that react and communicate this way, too. If they don't like what's happening, or sales figures are too low, you can almost count on the volume going up. If you make a mistake, it may mean the volcano is about to erupt. They react emotionally and communicate an environment of fear, hostility and intimidation. They try to control and manipulate you by way of their anger. They are counting on you not being comfortable in this environment and not liking confrontation. Because of that, they try to control and manipulate the situation by use of their anger, attitude and loud voice.

Instead of motivation, this tactic and communication style tends to alienate people, just as I talked about back in Chapter Two, The Challenges to Communication. This is an example of one of those challenges, a reason for disconnect. A parent may get angry and react this way, thinking if they scream or raise their voice, the child will listen. They don't. They get frustrated and tune parents out. Some things never change!

> *...When we are operating unconsciously out of a preference (our style) and not seeing the results we expect, we actually have a tendency to intensify our preferred behavior — even when it's not working!*
> — Harvard Business Review - 2012

D. The Past Is Never Past

Recently, I was working with two partners of a medium-sized business that is on the verge of explosive growth. That sounds like a good thing, right? Not necessarily. The principle partner, who was also the CEO, had an objective he wanted to see become a reality.

As I sat in the room and watched the dynamics between the two partners, I noticed the CEO. The more he thought his business partner didn't agree with him, the louder, more reactive, aggressive and forceful he became in how he tried to deliver his message.

He was not explaining his thought process with facts, rather he used emotions. When his business partner brought up issues and concerns with the direction the CEO wanted to go, the CEO responded with the litany of things the partner had done over the past two years the CEO perceived to be negative.

What this did was attempt to make the business partner abandon his concerns over the CEO's desired direction, as the partner now felt he needed to go on the defensive. In this way, by dragging up everything from the past, what really happened was to change the subject and move away from what the real issues were.

This can happen in personal relationships as well. When one person brings up something that happened in the past, it's an attempt to control the situation by starting a "Well, you did this..." in an attempt to gain back what is perceived as a loss of control in the conversation.

In giving the CEO this feedback later, he at first denied it, and then sat back, thought a minute, and although frustrated, said he knew I was right.

5. You're Thinking Like YOU!

All of us approach a situation from our own frame of reference, our own personality type and our own set of personal history books. Because of this, we expect everyone else to use our personal references as well.

Although we don't realistically expect everyone to think like us, when it comes to communication, we really do need to get over ourselves. Unfortunately, we are so programmed to think and react, speak and communicate like "us," we have a hard time when others don't.

Remember when you were in school? Your friends were people like you, who had similar interests as you, had a similar sense of humor, looked at life much the same way, and so on.

PART II AVOIDING TRAIN WRECKS AND STAYING ON TRACK

We are so caught up in ourselves sometimes, that we need to consciously take a moment before we respond/react or communicate to realize that others may be affected by the way, or *how* we say something.

When my husband and I had just gotten back from our honeymoon, we were back to work for the first time since the blessed event. My husband is very detailed, fact-based, to-the-point and logical. I'm very spontaneous, big-picture oriented and outgoing. You get the idea.

I decided it would be great to call him at work to tell him that I missed being away from him and couldn't wait to see him that night. I dialed his number and could feel the butterflies as the phone started to ring.

"Hello?" he said.
"Hi! It's ME," I gushed.
Expecting words of love, I heard him say, "Hi. What do you need?"
Need....... what do I NEED? I was crushed. I wanted him to say, "HI! I love you. I'm SO glad you called!"
I said, "Nothing,"
"I just wanted to say hi and see how it was going."
"Great," he said, "See you tonight." Click. Hmmph.

When he got home that evening, I shared a little "feedback" and told him how I felt. He apologized and told me that, at work, he's so busy and running so crazy all day that he's really focused the entire day.

The next time I called him, I started the conversation with, "Hi, I just have three things I need to ask you." I did get right to the point thinking he'd then hang up.

"I'm glad you called. How are you?" he asked.

Life was good! Now he was conscious of trying to communicate using my style, not his. I did the same. Wedded bliss.

We don't expect others to act like us just in personal conversations and relationships, but in professional ones, as well. The CEO of a mid-sized health-care company shared there were several challenges within the ranks of the executive leadership team. The three-person team was having issues. After doing some consulting and observing the team, I found the reason, in great part, was they were all thinking like themselves!

One of the team was a strong visionary, confident in his talents in determining the big picture and the direction the company should go. While the other two were also visionary, their strengths were in the details of how to get there. Emails were detailed, processes were discussed and documented. This worked well for the two of them. It even gave them commonalities that helped strengthen their working relationship.

The challenge came when they expected the third person to be like them and to be detailed also. Their definitions of "detailed" were very different. When I asked "the visionary" to send me an email to summarize a recent meeting, he sent a paragraph. When I asked the CEO to do the same thing, he sent an outlined page with subtopics. The differences in each other's expectations and communication styles were causing a lot of friction.

Each thought their way was right. We had to work through the differences in communication and realize that high level, or a lack of detailed information, is fine for conveying general information, while other pieces of communication need to have deeper explanations, and have details included and documented for others to follow processes and directions.

PART II AVOIDING TRAIN WRECKS AND STAYING ON TRACK

Otherwise, managers and leaders may set their teams up to fail, and not even realize it.

What you say, as well as *how* you say it, can have impact you may not even be aware of.

I have known and respected for many years the executive vice president of Human Resources for a major Fortune 100 company. I mentioned to her how much easier it must have been for her years ago: back then, when she responded to someone, it carried the same weight as anyone else. She didn't have to choose as carefully the words she used or how she said them, although she has always been conscientious in this area. Back then, she was one of many. Now, everything she says carries escalated weight. If she has a conversation with someone, many times, they're trying to read as much between the lines of what she's saying, as they are the lines themselves. In her position, *how* she says something is crucial.

As managers move into leadership with a company and their positions and opinions carry a greater and broader impact, everything they say can also have greater weight to those listening. While the manager might make a comment they don't give a second thought to, the person it was directed to may have a totally different perception. Because of the manager's position in the company, that small, and seemingly unimportant response, may make or break someone else's entire day.

> *The most important thing in communication is hearing what isn't said*
>
> — Peter F. Drucker: Austrian-born American management consultant, educator, and author

According to Kevin Eikenberry, who studied at Purdue and is an author, speaker and trainer, whenever someone becomes a new leader, that person goes through "Four Transitions to Leadership."

1. Relationships change
2. Roles change
3. Skills evolve (hopefully!)
4. Perspectives adjust

Just as I mentioned with the executive I've known and respected for many years, once she moved into executive leadership, not only did her role change, the way people related to her changed due to her new position, as well.

The Science of It All

If you're concerned that collaborating with some people may be hard to do, especially with someone you have a somewhat "negative" history with, or someone who has demonstrated one or more of the "Reasons for Disconnect" we talked about, before you can collaborate, you have to forgive. Why? Because you're "Thinking like You!" Yes, you heard me. Forgiveness is the only thing that will clear the meeting table so you can start fresh with that person who has wronged you. That creates the negative "history" that I talked about in the chapter on "Challenges in Communication." Forgiveness isn't easy to do. They may genuinely deserve the wrath of your feelings. However, it has also been scientifically proven, as long as we're talking about science here, to have positive, physical effects as well when you forgive someone.

Researchers at the Mayo Clinic (Google Search benefits of forgiveness January 28, 2014),

There are benefits from forgiving someone.

Letting go of grudges and bitterness can make way for compassion, kindness and peace. Forgiveness can lead to:

- Healthier relationships
- Greater spiritual and psychological well-being
- Less anxiety, stress and hostility
- Lower blood pressure
- Fewer symptoms of depression
- Lower risk of alcohol and substance abuse

So, what's one of the best ways to ensure you aren't the one generating the disconnect, or causing another person to misperceive your message? You must be aware that, It's not just what you say, "It's HOW You Say It"™

> *Forgiveness is a vulnerable act that can feel like it opens us up to more pain. But we need to have a way to process and let go of the effects of injury, or we risk serious physical and emotional consequences,*
> reports — Angela Haupt, US News and World Report, August 29, 2012

According to this report, experts in this field have done studies that show that people who decide to forgive someone who has, in our opinion, wronged us, have actual health benefits. For example, in those cases, the person who forgave found it helped lower blood pressure, cholesterol, and heart rate.

Direct Quote:
> "...forgiveness is associated with improved sleep quality, which has a strong effect on health. Duke University researchers report a strong correlation between forgiveness and strengthened immunity among HIV-positive patients. The benefits aren't just limited to the physical, either: Letting go of old grudges reduces levels of depression, anxiety, and anger. People who forgive tend to have better relationships, feel happier and more optimistic, and overall, enjoy better psychological well-being."

All Aboard

Although not always comfortable, if you follow the rule to forgive and forget, how can that benefit your health as well as your outlook? How can that bring back the passion you had for your work? Rules and passion. Hmm. Odd combination? It sounds like an oxymoron. Rules bring to mind structure, constraint and boredom. Passion, just the opposite: Wild abandon and unfettered emotion -- fragrance commercials!

I wondered how these two live together? What occurred to me is that rules give your passions the freedom to be more intense, more passionate! In my profession, keynote speaking and corporate training, there are also rules to follow: Engage your audience and provide valuable content. The audience members come in as if they're on a runaway train. They don't really know where they're going or how to get there. I take them safely on the journey with me, building a picture of where I'm taking them! A picture of somewhere they'd love to be. I let them see how their careers will be better because of the trip they're taking with me.

What is the source in me that conjures passion? It's the adrenaline rush of seeing the audience, knowing they're there to see me, and knowing that I'm going to help change their business, as well as, personal relationships. When I can feel they're "with me," it makes me feel exhilarated and alive. It's like being the conductor on a speeding train -- fully in control, yet running, full force toward a great destination.

Think about the rules you need to follow in your management position. Do you still feel the passion you once did, or have the rules overtaken it? Take a minute to sit in a quiet place. No one else around. Make a list of those things that you were passionate about when you first started. Look at the list. Are you still passionate about them? Do the rules you follow support the passion, or make it more difficult? Think about it.

Passion can also increase emotion. Read the book by David Caruso and Peter S. Alovey from Yale, *Emotionally Intelligent Managers-How to Develop and Use the Four Key Emotional Skills of Leadership.*

How can passion and rules live together? Blending them can take you from "The Little Engine That Could" to the "Freedom Train." All Aboard!

CHAPTER FOUR

The 6-Step "It's HOW You Say It"™ Principle for Effective Communication

In the preceding chapters we've talked about the reasons people may misunderstand your message. Misunderstandings are based upon many variables, from your history with that person or group to the way you've delivered the information.

In this chapter, I'll share how to lessen the chances the conversation may be misperceived. The most important thing to remember "It's Not Just What You Say," in effective communication, "It's HOW You Say It"™

It's HOW You Say It™

The 6-Step
...It's HOW You Say It℠
Principle

The principle consists of the following steps:

Step 1: Ask and Suggest
Step 2: Check Your Facial Expressions and Body Language
Step 3: Be Aware of Your Tone of Voice
Step 4: Show Value in Their Ideas
Step 5: Give Kudos
Step 6: Be Real

Organizations have moved to flatter, leaner work teams, management teams and are also slimming down the number of people who hold upper leadership positions. When this happens, it's even more critical to have the power of positive influence and effective persuasion, especially if you're leading in a matrix situation. These six steps become essential in today's business environment.

Step 1: Ask and Suggest

Sometimes we look only at the surface of situations and look at issues or projects through our own lenses. Remember that being in a leadership position, or being in a position where you believe you can be a leader, doesn't mean intimidating people or telling them what to do. Instead, making suggestions, not demands, and asking, when you need to have something done, as if you were asking someone for a favor will be interpreted as collaborative and not controlling. How you phrase your request is important. Clear, yet positive and polite, directives will be the most productive. For instance, if your teams send in a monthly or weekly report, rather than telling them they have five days to get it submitted, ask them to submit it by the fifth day. "I need to ask that you have your reports in by Friday afternoon. If you could get them to me sooner, that would be great. [Then give your reasons.] I need to roll up the information from them and have it to Mary by Monday. If I could get them earlier than Friday, I may be able to get a start on them before the weekend. I'd really appreciate that."

The difference between telling them to do it and asking them to do it is huge although you may feel it insignificant. I have found in my research and experiences in many large Fortune 50 - 500 companies, as well as medium-sized businesses, the leaders who are confident and self-assured don't need to throw their authority around to establish their position. They use their approach to build teams up, not tear them down. They don't try to frighten people or speak forcefully; they collaborate and consider themselves a part of the team, not above it. They ask and suggest, not tell and demand.

This type of approach does something more important than make the people on the team feel more relaxed: it builds respect. Show respect to everyone, at every level, of the organization. In doing so, you are establishing not only a stronger relationship at that moment, you are also modeling the behavior at a leadership level that shows this is the behavior you expect everyone to demonstrate, and the way everyone should treat each other regardless of their positions within the organization. If you're in a position of authority, know that whatever you say and however you act, is taken more to heart, more seriously, than if people were hearing the same information from someone else.

Many years ago, one of the Fortune 100 companies I worked with relocated me to Dallas, Texas. At the time, the corporate offices were in Manhattan in New York. One of the best examples of "suggesting" that I have experienced in my career, was here.

Dallas happened to be one of the four major area headquarters across the country. Because of this, I was also in the same office as the area director. This man was in charge of a quarter of the United States. Everything that happened in that geographic area rolled upward to him as well: All sales, marketing, financials, product, training and development. He was a politically powerful person. While he had his quirks, I'll never forget the way he always acted as though my opinions were valuable. He never tried to make me feel insignificant or foolish.

Back in those days, when I used to come up with an idea, in my excitement, I'd run right to his office. I would go right past the assistant, not bothering to stop and ask if he was busy. I knew he'd be thrilled to hear the brilliant thought I'd had.

One particular day, I had come up with an idea for a new brand extension that I thought, at the time, was just a stroke of genius, and I knew, of course, he'd want to know right away. I went right in and he was looking down at his paperwork. He stopped, didn't raise his head, but just looked over his wire-rimmed half-glasses at me. "Don't let Debbie [the administrative assistant] stop you, she's just there for show," and he smiled.

"I know you're busy, but I came up with an idea that's really good, and I thought you'd want to hear it," I babbled. "Can't wait" was his reply. By the time I finally ran out of air and came up for a breath I couldn't wait to hear his thoughts. He looked at me with a question mark on his expression. Rather than tell me that was the dumbest thing he'd ever heard, what he said was something to this effect. "Hmm, that sounds like it may have merit. Tell me how 'this' will work." I'd flounder a little bit, never having thought of 'that.' He did that about four or five times... with great interest in the answer. Finally, I said to him, "That's the dumbest idea I've ever heard." He smiled.

His words of wisdom to me were: "If you can shoot holes in your own ideas, and anticipate what others may find in them as cracks, and they still hold water, you have something." It would have been easy for him to shoot me down, tell me what to do with the idea, and ask me to leave. He never made me feel my ideas were bad, or dumb. He would have crushed that excitement I had for the company and the brand. Instead of coming down with his position power and telling me what to do, he made suggestions. If he would step into a meeting I was in, and listen to the outcomes, every now and then, he'd make a suggestion. We acted on everything he said. Not because he told us we HAD to but because we valued the way he approached it and knew his knowledge and focus was the right way to go.

He was like a business coach. He led us in the direction we should go, gave us the tools and equipment to be successful and then encouraged us to go out and "play our best."

Lou Hollz, the well-known football coach at Notre Dame, was an excellent coach. He was also famous for his extremely successful leadership style, a style that was easy for his players to follow. He built all his teams with three values:

- Do what's right.
- Do your best.
- Treat others the way you want to be treated.

(Source: "Business Values: What Standards Help Your Team Work Together and Actually Enjoy Doing it?" Program developed by Joe Calhoon, National Speaker)

So, by being a great leadership example in your character, you are helping to build a great team environment. By demonstrating the "It's HOW You Say It"™ Principle starting with asking and suggesting instead of telling, you also help to build trust. You are relating to them with respect and as an equal instead of using your authority and position to tell them what to do.

Many managers or supervisors may not realize they are telling people what to do, and it's coming across negatively and harshly. There are others who do this, and communicate in such a way, that they intentionally do tell people what to do. They feel it raises their authority and position power.

Consistent with my observations and research, it's the leaders that act as though everyone is more important than they are that are actually revered in their role as an inspiring leader.

Whatever you feel your strengths and talents are, use those to help the people in your environment who you manage, or the team you are a part of. If we use those gifts as a sledge hammer, they are not doing much good!

When talking about people President Abraham Lincoln suggested

> *Persuade rather than coerce.*
> *A good leader avoids issuing orders,*
> *preferring to request,*
> *imply or make suggestions.*
> — Donald T. Philips, author of, *Lincoln on Leadership: Executive Strategies for Tough Times*

Step 2. Check Your Facial Expressions and Body Language

This may not be as obvious and simple as it seems. How you are feeling on the inside shows itself on the outside. If you're upset, disappointed, tired or disengaged, it shows on the outside. You may not think it does, but if your face doesn't say "I'm here and glad to be," it can have a negative effect on everyone around you.

Remember when I mentioned the person that brightens the room by walking into it, and the person who brightens it by walking out? Which one are you? If it's the latter, you can bring down the feelings of everyone else around the table. It also sends a less-than-desireable message to the leadership at the table as well.

In psychology, there is a theory entitled the "facial feedback" hypothesis. This hypothesis states that "involuntary facial movements provide sufficient peripheral information to drive emotional experience." Marcia Purse blogs about this in "What's in a Smile? Expression Affects Emotion" as it relates to health issues and wellness.

The authors of another study, accomplished psychology educators S.F. Davis and J.J. Palladino, wrote that "feedback from facial expression affects emotional expression and behavior." In simple terms, you may actually be able to improve your mood by simply smiling!

When you smile at someone, and they smile back, the way they respond to you is due to 'mirror neurons' in your brain. These neurons are the brain's way of knowing what other people are intending and what they are feeling. These help you to determine how you should react to that person. Collaborate or cause trouble!

To take that a step further, David Rock, author of *Your Brain at Work,* explains when you interconnect your thoughts, emotions and goals with other people, you release oxytocin, a pleasurable chemical. It's the same chemical experience that a small child gets when he makes physical contact with his mother, from the moment of birth onward. Oxytocin is released when two people dance together, play music together, or engage in collaborative conversation.

Take a look inside. Do you like what you see? Are you happy to be in your position? Do you believe in the company and the mission it has set? If not, you may not be leading sincerely, and that can show itself on the outside.

This doesn't mean you have to go around smiling all day. As a matter-of-fact, that could be worse than not smiling enough. Take Jimmy Carter, for example. Some believe a factor in his election loss was he smiled too much, came across as insincere and people didn't trust him! What this means is, be aware that your facial expressions, as well as your body language, affects others.

When I worked in a major telecommunications company, our director had his office down the hall from mine. I truly thought the man disliked me. Each day he would walk down the hall and not even look at me. We came within mere feet of each other. I kept watching to see if he would just give me a small smile, or some indication, I wasn't on the "out" list. When I left that company, I asked him if I could talk with him briefly. I went into his office and shared what I had experienced and how it made me feel. He had a blank stare on his face. He thanked me for sharing and said he had no idea he was coming across that way. He explained that he was usually either coming out of a meeting, or going to his next meeting. Because of that, he told me he was moving with purpose and thinking about the action items from the meeting he'd just left, or thinking and anticipating what was going to happen in the next meeting. He apologized and told me he truly never "saw" anyone. He was that focused. He thanked me and said he really appreciated me sharing. He also assured me that he would be more aware and try to remember to look up as he was going to and from.

The next time you're in a meeting, take a look around the room. You'll be able to tell at a glance, who is interested, who is checked out and who is there because they have to be. Look at their posture. Who is engaged with their arms on the table? Who is engaged and taking notes? Who has their eye contact centered and focused on the person speaking? Who has their arms folded tightly, their legs crossed and not directly facing the table? Is anyone staring ahead blankly, not listening, just like when you were back in school, wondering when the bell would sound and you could escape?

What does your facial expression and body language say when you are conducting the meeting yourself or delivering a presentation? What your expressions and body language communicate to the participants determines their acceptance of you, in part, and their tendency to, in turn, accept or be open to the ideas you are presenting. Is the presentation for a client or a leader in your organization? In that case, the stakes are high and the positive outcome is critical. Your expressions, movements, gestures and a host of other things that seem very insignificant can make or break your audience's response.

Recently, I was helping a Fortune 500 corporation with one of their middle-level managers. She was on a great career path and wanted to move up. They realized her potential and wanted to get guidance for her. While she knew her subject matter inside and out, her audience would not have received the message because of the way she delivered it. She thought she was doing fine. I taped her doing an initial piece of it. Then we worked together, I pointed out several areas, let her try the skills and then taped again. She was amazed at the difference and said she didn't realize HOW she was delivering was greatly, and negatively, impacting what she was delivering. Although the many changes were, for the most part, subtle, the impact was significant.

In my presentations workshop, I go through a model I've created using the acronym S.P.E.A.K. that we talked about back in Chapter One (Stand on your own two feet - Professionalism, Passion, Presence - Engage - Action/Audience - Keep it Real/ Knowledge). Each letter of this acronym represents a strategy to follow and an action item for speaking in front of a live audience. The program is designed to help people who are delivering presentations get the support they need to have their audiences engage, not disengage.

The pioneer researcher on body language, Professor Albert Mehrabian of UCLA, (Nonverbal Communication 1972) revealed, what Karen L. Anderson, communication strategist, calls the "3V's." The impact of a message is about 7% Verbal (words and their meaning), 38% Vocal (including inflections, tone of voice and other vocal sounds) and 55% Visual, (including metaphors, images, graphics, colors, and design).

Additionally, communication researcher and anthropologist Ray Birdwhistell, founder of the field of kinesics (the interpretation of body language, facial expressions and gestures, and non-verbal behavior related to movement) estimated that an average person uses verbal communication for around 10 to 11 minutes a day, an average sentence taking only 2.5 seconds. Birdwhistell further estimated we can make and recognize around 250,000 facial expressions.

PART II   AVOIDING TRAIN WRECKS AND STAYING ON TRACK

Your interpretation of those nonverbals, body language and facial expressions may vary from person to person. Actually, your impression of how you interpret the signals may differ from the person standing right next to you who sees the exact same thing you are looking at, yet has a different impression of what message is being conveyed. Why?

It goes back to our chapter on The Reasons for Disconnect:

1. Our History Together
2. Appearances
3. Different Personalities
4. "He and She"
5. Agendas in the workplace
6. Your reputation
7. Do I Care

Body language and facial expression aren't just important at the meeting table. If you are having a conversation with someone at the office, or someone in your personal life, do they feel valued and respected by the unspoken signals you are giving? That may seem like a strange question when having a casual conversation. However, show respect to everyone. From the leaders of the corporation, to the entry level person. The question is, "Are you?"

Step 3. Be Aware of Your Tone of Voice

To me, tone is paramount in business and personal relationships. While you may not have intentionally used a disrespectful tone of voice, it is often the cause for conflict with people you live with or have personal relationships with, as well as people in an office environment. While you also may not think there's anything wrong with the way you say something, what's important is, would someone else say there is? In corporate or business environments, you may be more subtle. Just the slight edge to your voice, or, as often the case, a touch of sarcasm in your voice. "Sure we can try that. I'm sure that will work well."

Just as damaging is the tone of voice that comes with an attitude. That attitude comes across in your tone of voice, whether you feel it does or not. You may have the little voice in your head saying things you don't think the other person can hear. "Wow, look at Dana's shirt. I wonder if he owns an iron? I wonder if he's ever used it? He usually looks like he's just rolled out of bed." Those negative thoughts can come across in the tone of voice you use and be much more damaging than the words you are actually saying.

Think about the best relationships you have. The tone of voice you use with those people is, most probably, supportive, upbeat and respectful. Think of the people you don't have such good relationships with. Your conversations and communications with them are probably stilted, distrustful, guarded and stressful.

Don't forget that tone of voice can come across in email and texts as well. If you are the type of person that wants to have everything "documented," that sends the message you don't trust the other person, and maybe you don't! There may even be a warranted reason for that mistrust. Remember though, that when you send communication through email or text, it is even more important to guard the "tone" of your message. It's much easier for those to come across as cold and impersonal. That's not a great way to build a relationship.

Keep in mind that your best and your worst relationships are, in great part, a result of the way you communicate. "HOW

You Say It," has instant ramifications on building that history log mentioned back in the reasons for disconnect.

You may also have, at times, the personality I'll call "The Steamroller." This is the person who feels the right way is always their way. They have a force to their tone of voice. It's an authority to it that, they hope, will have you fall in line to their way of thinking. This tone of voice may be a little intimidating. If your self-confidence isn't up where it needs to be, you may feel you have to follow their directions because their message is delivered with a tone of "force" to it. Some people use the tone of their voice as a way to manipulate you. In a business situation, it may be someone in a leadership position, or can just as easily be a counterpart or even a direct report. This happens in personal relationships as well. Someone may even be uncomfortable having conversations. In order get around that, they try to control you, even subtly, by trying to manipulate your decisions and choices by their tone of voice.

The opposite is also a call for caution. Be sure you are not one of those who can't seem to make a decision, and it shows in your tone of voice. Many times we're afraid of making a wrong decision. Because of that, our tone of voice tends to sound "wishy-washy." For instance, if someone says, "What do you think of X?" Rather than give a confident answer and make a mistake, you tend to give an answer that is more of a question. If the other person disagrees, you may be quick to change your mind and say you were "almost going to say that" and then turn to their way of thinking.

Do you sound as if you aren't really sure about anything? Do you think people will think less of you if you give an answer they don't like or agree with? Read through the last few paragraphs. Does your voice give that impression? Remember the Communication Components we talked about in Chapter One? Raising your voice at the end of a sentence is how some people speak. Their tone of voice diminishes credibility because it goes up at the end of every sentence; whether they're asking a question or not. I have coached many people on this.

Know that you are not able to change other people. That would make the world a much easier place. Unfortunately, we only have control over ourselves. While you may not be able to change the way they deliver their message, you can change how you react and respond to it.

Just as off-putting as the forceful tone of voice, or the wishy-washy communicator, is the voice of impatience. When someone comes to ask you something and you give the impression that you have fifty important things to do and whoever is interrupting you isn't any of them, it gives the message to them that you don't care and they aren't important. That makes the "communication teeter-totter" we talked about back in Chapter Two lean way to the negative side.

That's not to say that you can, or should, drop everything when someone walks into your office. There are times you do have priorities and need to follow through on them. If that's the case, how you say that to someone makes the difference between whether they walk away satisfied, or walk away steaming.

If someone comes to your office and you truly can't talk with them at that time, share it with them respectfully, and sincerely that you aren't able to talk, a brief reason why and suggest an alternative. "I'm sorry, I have just a short time to get ready for 'X' and am not able to talk right now. I do want to hear what you have to say or find out what I can help you with and want to make sure you have my full time and attention.

I should be open this afternoon around 2:00. Are you able to stop by then?" Unfortunately, in a business environment, you may not know the impact your tone of voice may have, but the other team members may because you might just be the topic of discussion for the next week.

Tone of voice also plays a major factor when you, or the other person, has a much higher degree of expertise in a subject. For instance, say Mickie is in the healthcare field, or technologies. If Mickie is talking with someone else, trying to share information and they ask her a question, if they don't understand her answer right away, or it's information that Mickie feels they should already know, her tone of voice may take on a slightly negative or condescending tone.

Whether you realize it or not, it has a strong impact on the relationship. They see you not as a leader, or someone who can help, but as an antagonist. The opposite is sometimes true with the same scenario. You don't act condescendingly towards them, you act with a hint of superiority. It's almost as if "I know this and you don't."

When I first started in telecom, the entire world seemed like an acronym. I think the only reason there are so many acronyms in those fields is so that it can make the people that know what they all mean feel cool. I actually heard someone ask a very simple question once. Instead of answering the question simply, the respondent went out of his way to use every "$10 word" he could to make himself sound cool. When he was met with a blank stare from the person that asked, I think he was pleased he was able to show off. When I then answered the question simply, she smiled and said, "Is that the same thing he just said?" Yes, it was. If you want to build relationships and trust within your organization, be the example of humility. Be the answer to a problem, not the cause of another one!

Step 4. Show Value in Their Ideas

Everyone likes to feel as though they have something of value to contribute to conversations, as well as organizations. Cutting someone off before they have fully explained an idea, or showing in your facial expressions that this won't work or you want to move on, is one sure way to damage that relationship.

Just like the leader in Dallas allowed me to rant on about my half-baked idea, it would have been much easier, and faster, for him to cut me off and tell me he was busy. He knew that the excitement I had for the position and the company was something that, once snuffed out, would be hard, if not impossible, to get back.

Think about the people in your organizations. You can teach products, procedures, etc. You can't teach motivation. If you have a person who's motivated, take care and build that relationship to help them reach their great potential. One way to do that is to show value in their ideas.

This doesn't mean that you have to use all their ideas, or even like them. It means that you build that relationship by listening to them, asking questions about how it would work and, when appropriate, give it a try! This can be an idea for a project, it can be an idea for what to do with a team builder, it can even be inviting them to a focus group or brain-storming session. Including someone in a lunch invitation, as well as asking them to participate in a project that has high visibility within the organization, or to the executive leadership team, is a great step. According to Dale Carnegie and Zig Ziglar, allowing someone to feel included is so important to building the team. Although no words are spoken when you are showing inclusion, it speaks volumes as to how you value the relationship.

Many years ago I had a new manager who was a great friend of the person who hired him. In her eyes, he could do no wrong. I had management experience and he didn't. I think he felt slightly intimidated. He had two friends that were on our team. I had taken a huge step back in my career at the time to join this team. Our daughter was an infant and I wanted to get off the road and not travel. When offered this position, at the time, I thought it was a great solution.

We worked in a pod environment. About three times a week, this manager would come into the pod, look at his two friends and announce out loud that he wanted them to go to lunch with him. They would look at the young woman who sat with them and ask her, too. When the entire group trooped out of the room together, I was both a little hurt not to be invited, and glad they were gone! Even though I may not have gone often, being invited would have gone a long way to building the group. As a clarification, a group is not a team because I wasn't included. I was only there a year, though and decided I had to "move back up." When you demonstrate that you don't value the person, it's clear you don't value their ideas as well.

Step 5. Give Kudos

Affirming, when warranted, isn't only a good way to build a team, it's the right thing to do. When given sincerely, not only does it say to the person that they are valued and appreciated, it also lets them know you recognize their time and are aware of their efforts.

> *Nothing else can quite substitute for a few well-chosen, well-timed, sincere words of praise.*
>
> **Sam Walton**
> **Founder of Walmart**

Praise, however, is best in small doses (notice Sam Walton mentions a 'few' well-chosen words). You bestow praise upon someone. Be aware of the difference though, between affirmation and praise. When you affirm someone, it enables them to recognize their own value and self-worth. "Debbie, you have great ideas." Praise is more of a judgement. It can lead to negatives as well as positives, depending upon the health of that relationship. "Good job on the report, Carl."

When you give kudos, this is also a really important time to take a look inside yourself. Are you giving recognition to the same people each time? If the history with that person isn't strong, do you tend to look for the wrong they do, instead of the right.

If you are a parent, or have nieces and nephews, people caution that people tend to look for the negative and try to correct it, rather than the positive, and try to reinforce it. Be aware of the tendency to do that with employees you don't feel are doing as well as they should.

Do you work in a matrix environment, or have direct reports in other cities? Are you aware of what they consider a reward? Although you can't be there in person often, do you make sure to keep in touch with them? Often, keeping communication open and saying, "Hi" when you don't want anything at all can build trust, as well as the relationship.

In Ken Blanchard's book, *Situational Leadership II*, he cautions against being a "seagull manager." A seagull manager is one that swoops in, makes a lot of noise, dumps a load on everyone and then flies out! If you call your folks, or stop by their offices and their reaction is they're waiting for the "load" to fall, you may want to reassess how, and why, you usually interact with them. If you only show up when you want to let them know when they've done something wrong, or something's past due, you are filling the role of the "seagull manager." It's important for people to know that when you come around, they don't have to be afraid. It should be a good thing to have management and leadership accessible.

Conversation with someone, just for the sake of saying "Hi," and building the relationship can be reinforcing. Make a point to communicate and have a conversation even when there is nothing you need from them.

In working with a very large cable company, I was impressed by how visible their senior leadership is. In the business services division, the field sales team in a certain division loves it when their VP comes. Why? It's fun. The VP picks one sales person. He goes into the field with them and cold calls. He takes one side of the street, the rep the other. They have a time limit and see who can make more sales. It's a great competition. At the end of the day, bragging rights are in order. Did they outsell the VP? The good news is, all sales the VP made still go to the rep. The VP buys his/her lunch and shares things he heard and saw to build the rep up, reinforce their hard work and thank them for a fun day. He also answers any questions they may have and offers suggestions as well.

Although giving kudos may sound like something that would be common sense, think about the last time you made a point to make someone feel appreciated. Was it done in the way that made them feel good?

When I was an entry level sales rep, I had wonderful numbers. I would get recognized by my manager in a team meeting, and I loved it. That's because my personality type is an extrovert who loves the limelight! Other people who are shy or don't like to have attention drawn to them may see that as a negative. If you aren't sure how people like to be recognized, ask them!

I was asked to consult with a large firm on a sales excellence program. We were in a room having one of the first meetings when several of the managers started talking about what they should use as "rewards" for great sales performance. They threw out all these ideas and looked at me to see my reaction. When I didn't show a reaction, they asked me, "What do you think we should use as the rewards?" "It depends," I said, "Have you asked them what they'd like?" They looked at each other with blank stares as if that was a foreign concept.

Although you would think that money or time off are the only motivators, think again. One of the large cable corporations that I work with found a wonderful way to give kudos that had nothing to do with giving time off or money. Once a year, there was a sales competition between two divisions. The bar was set high. Each team tried to outdo the other. It was based upon numbers from all team members so that not just the "stars" were able to sway numbers. Whichever team won, the other team had to go the winner's office, don aprons and bring electric griddles and make the other team's breakfast in front of the entire office. They love it. It got to be a tradition and the coveted "Pancake Awards" were born. The winning team sat at a big conference table, usually with fork and knife in hand just to rub it in. The manager of the losing team, bought pancake mix, syrup, and juice. The losing sales team made the breakfast, set the table, did the dishes and presented them with the "trophy." In essence, what it amounted to, was a year of bragging rights. The leadership from the division came in and had breakfast too and said a few words to the winning team. It was great.

Step 6. Be Real

After all is said and done, people aren't going to know if it's "Step 1" you're trying to do or if you made a mistake trying out "Step 3." What they will know, are you being "real?" Are you being yourself and are you sincere? If you make a mistake, apologize; if they walk into a room, have a smile. Try looking at the world through the work glasses they wear every day. Are you the answer to a problem or the source of another problem?

As you grew up, you lived and worked by "The Golden Rule," and treated people the way you wanted to be treated. We have now become sensitized to The Platinum Rule in the work place and should treat people how they would like to be treated. Either rule, the premise is to treat people with respect. It can solve a host of problems. Honesty is not only the best policy, it's the right thing to do. Do they know you have their best interests at heart? Are you there to support and help them, or are you there to hover over them and come down hard if they make a mistake?

Look at the work group, if I were to ask them if you have any favorites on the team, what would they say? It doesn't matter what you would say, what's important is how they feel.

Be the person that brightens the room by walking into it, not out of it. Look at what "can" work instead of what can't.

Your reputation is important. Build it with respect, honesty and kindness. Why? While you have to be good at what you do and knowledgeable in your field, people will never forget if you climbed over them or through them to get to where you are.

In one company I worked with, there were a lot of office politics between the areas across the country. People weren't known for the kindness they showed each other, it was almost the opposite. Leaders tended to build their own individual kingdoms and ruled within them. When the economy warranted it, corporate decided to consolidate and started to reorganize the areas down from six to four. Needless-to-say, this wasn't a good thing for many of the people who had ruled with an iron fist, or hadn't been too concerned with how they had treated people. One of the national chain account managers, as a joke, sent out bridge building kits to folks in those areas. Everyone got a great laugh out of it, and the point was driven home.

This is the most important: Go by the Golden Rule and treat people the way you want to be treated. Be kind to those above you, beside you and below you. Someone below you may be your manager someday! This can do so much. If you walk in to someone's office, and their first thought is "What did I do wrong now?", you're not around enough for the right reasons. Ask people how their weekends were, share a small piece of your weekend. For goodness sake, smile. Realize in the scheme of life, this is one day and the only chance you have to make a positive impact on someone's life today.

HOW you say something can make a V.A.S.T. difference in your relationships: When you follow the 6-Step r relationships: When ™ Principle, it can have a positive impact on relationships and leave people feeling:

V - Valued
< or >?

These symbols, less than (<) or greater than (>) are the same ones you used to see in math class. If you've made others feel < you, it creates a negative relationship and makes them feel undervalued and uncomfortable being around you as though they don't matter. This is an attempt to make them feel as if they are a lower status than you. If you put on a little humility, making them feel > you, you may have given them a gift that can significantly strengthen this relationship. Everyone has a need to feel valued and accepted. Is there a value to the company in doing this as well?

According to Forbes, in 1992, Harvard Business School Professors James Heskett and John Kotter completed an extensive research project detailing the corporate cultures of 200 companies and how each company's culture affected its long-term economic performance. Their book, *Corporate Culture and Performance*, argued that strong corporate cultures that facilitate adaptation to a changing world are associated with strong financial results. They found that those cultures highly value employees, customers, and owners and that those cultures encourage leadership from everyone in the firm. So if customer needs change, a firm's culture almost forces people to change their practices to meet the new needs. And anyone, not just a few people, is empowered to do just that.

This same study, done by John Kotter and James Heskett, discovered the profits of an organization skyrocketed when the organization's culture valued ALL stakeholders, internal, external as well as shareholders. Profits were 756% higher than other companies that didn't have those traits. The study concluded that performance excellence is tied to valuing all stakeholders, not just shareholders.

> *Serving the needs of all stakeholders in business may require a little humility but ultimately it reaps great rewards.*
> -- Barbara Teicher

A - Appreciated and Accepted

Are their contributions being recognized? Do you give credit where credit is due for all the hard work they've put in? Do they know you don't take them for granted? Do you? Do you tend to dump more work on those you know can get the job done yet give a lighter load to those you don't have as much confidence in?

I asked a manager once if he told his direct reports he appreciated the time and effort they were putting in on a certain project. He asked me why he should thank them for doing their job. He said that's why they got paid. Wouldn't you love to work for him?

S - Secure

Has HOW you've communicated with someone built the relationship so they feel secure with you? Have you avoided the reasons that make people feel disconnected from you? Have you used a supportive tone of voice? Have you been yourself with them so they don't feel you're putting on airs or being insincere? Have you shown them respect? Security will come from all these areas. Security also has to do with the team. Have you made them feel secure in their team? Do you have,

T - Trusted

If you don't have trust in a relationship, they will never feel valued. Have you shown that you won't try to blindside or undermine them? Do you trust them? Can they tell by the ways you communicate whether you do or not? If they tell you something in confidence, whether you agree with them or not, as long as it isn't something that may give insight to a dangerous situation, do you keep that confidence to yourself?

Have you demonstrated integrity? Integrity builds trust. Do you lead by example and make sure they know the values you expect them to model on a daily basis?

"How You Say It"™ can make a V.A.S.T. difference. Both in your business as well as your personal relationships. People want to feel valued, appreciated, secure and trusted.

> *I've learned that people will forget what you said, people will forget what you did, but people will never forget how you made them feel.*
> — Maya Angelou

Three Beliefs:
1. I believe a well-spoken word has the power to instill confidence, motivation, loyalty and a host of other sought-after qualities — or it can just as easily damage relationships, deflate dreams and crush the spirit.

> **2. I believe the essential skill sets of leadership can be taught, and the true essence of leadership is a mindset.**
>
> **3. I believe telling the truth and conducting business, and your life, with integrity shouldn't be for the benefit of others who are watching but for the benefit of a restful night's sleep and the ability to look into the mirror and be proud of who you see.**
>
> — Barbara Teicher

The Science of It All

According to David Rock, a neuroscientist who has done extensive work and research on the brain, "A feeling of relatedness is a primary reward for the brain and an absence of relatedness generates primary threat." When you have a good relationship with that person, no "history" you're dealing with, and you aren't experiencing any of the "Reasons for Disconnect" as in Chapter Two.

In a study on social pain conducted in 2008, the findings revealed that social pain comes back when you think about it again, whereas physical pain does not. Think about that. True!

All Aboard
Are You Making a V.A.S.T. Difference? - The Checklist

PART II AVOIDING TRAIN WRECKS AND STAYING ON TRACK

In the last month have you	YES	NO	V.A.S.T.	Describe it
Intentionally made a point to say or do something to make someone at a lower level feel valued?			Valued	
Supported someone's suggestion by asking for more info - not discounting it. Thanked them, sincerely, for the idea, making them feel part of the team?			Accepted and Appreciated	
Evenly distributed higher visibility projects, not only to your go-to people, and set them up for success?			Secure	
Had a heart-to-heart with someone on your team asking how it's going. Confirmed with them what their leadership goals are? Offered your suggestions from your experience of the best path to take and how to get there?			*Trusted*	

Take a minute to think about your personal life. What have you done in the last month to make a V.A.S.T. difference in your relationships?

V	
A	
S	
T	

PART III
NAVIGATING THE STATIONS & SIDETRACKS TO REACH YOUR DESTINATION

You are the force behind the Leadership locomotive. You are making a V.A.S.T. difference in the lives of those who have caught the train. You are chugging into the station. Are you sure you've been steaming towards the right destination? Will your train survive and will you still shine with excitement?

CHAPTER FIVE

True Leadership - How to Become the Difference

Along the course of your career journey, you've moved up the tracks. In some cases, from the caboose all the way to where you are now -- you fuel the engine. You have the power to move the train wherever you want it to go. You are, finally, the engineer. You've probably been derailed a few times along the way. You've had to change tracks and have switched stations as well. That only stoked your engine's fire and made you more determined to get to your ultimate destination.

While the train metaphor is strong here, the focus should remain on the impact you are building as a leader. What kind of legacy are you building?

Question: Are you on the right track? Are you speeding forward, yet the lone whistle in the night? Are you stoking your fire, yet, if you truly think about it, the fire is only in you?

The question isn't do you know where you're taking the train. There are really two questions now: 1) are you stoking the fires in all the different teams whose contributions are needed to keep the entire train racing, and 2) do your teams want to go the same places you do? If you arrive at your destination, and you've made it in record time, if there's no one else on board, what difference will it make?

According to *The Persuasive Leader*, Harvard Business Press, there are Four Levels of Leadership Influence:
1) <u>Compliance</u>: Laws, policies, procedures - Your teams will follow these because there are consequences to avoid
2) <u>Transaction</u>: Just do it because it's just easier to do this than not.
3) <u>Transference</u>: The person who can begin to make the difference as we talked about in earlier chapters can influence others by this person's nature, character, and other attributes. Transference is likely to get derailed during periods of anxiety within the organization. That's because during these times people tend to think and act more emotionally than normal. They may have higher feelings of insecurity and fear. They may need to be reaffirmed more often than normal because of the uncertainty that's going on around them. It's like the need to be given reinforcement from your mom and dad when you were a child.
4) <u>Transformation</u>: The ultimate influence when the leader's values align with the organization and the followers. Teams are all aboard and the speeding train is efficient and well-tuned.

Here is a critical question: What are your values? Think about it carefully. Does success, as society defines it, matter? You now have, what you thought was the ultimate. It's what you've spent countless hours trying to achieve: the position, the status, the money, the power. When it comes down to it, those who are in these elite positions, thrive on the power. Money is a great perk, it's the symbol of what's important, but it's not what fuels the train.

PART III   NAVIGATING THE STATIONS & SIDETRACKS TO REACH YOUR DESTINATION

The challenge is, if we want to continue to ride this train, we need to make sure that everyone who works on, rides on, and has stock in this particular train, not only likes the destination, but is eager to get there. Do you REALLY want to continue this trip?

When we get to this level of power, do we understand what it has really cost us? What does that mean?

> ***"What Price Glory?"***
> **— The famous play by Maxwell Anderson and Laurence Stallings asks the question, "What Price Glory Now?"**

Power comes at a price. Just as a circuit will blow if too much power is pulled at once, so does our life. As we chug the uphill battle to "make it," we make conscious decisions along the way. We travel often, work long hours and sacrifice a lot, sometimes our own health, in the name of having the most high-powered, prestigious and lucrative position. Others may admire us. That feels good and boosts the ego.

When you look in the mirror though, whom do you see? When you go home at night, whatever time that ends up being, who's there? Is there someone there? If there's someone there, are they glad to see you, or do they tolerate you being there until you leave again? Do you ever feel alone in a room full of people? I don't mean the ones who want to be seen by you; I'm talking about the ones who you truly like and care about and you want to be around.

What do you really want? If you were gone tomorrow, would years go by before they replaced you? Months? Weeks?

Society says we should have it all. I'll have the house, the car, the family and the image. If I have these "things," I must truly be happy and successful. Right? When you are finally home, are you still working? Are you still connected to the station? Are you derailed when you aren't doing something for the company for more than a day and feel a little lost? Do you thrive on that frantic pace? Many executives reach the pinnacle of their careers by sacrificing themselves and the relationships with their families and loved ones.

As mentioned in a previous chapter, my husband covers an NFL team for a national sports network. Many years ago, he had become friends with one of the coaches who was here at the time. The coach, dedicated to his career and well-known throughout the NFL as being great at what he did, was on the field at practice one day. He noticed a young man on the sidelines and thought how smart and engaged he was. He thought that kid would have a great career because of his young enthusiasm. It didn't hit him right away: it was his own son. He didn't know his son was there. It made him sad that it took him that long to recognize his own son because the coach was away from home so much.

How do you handle the power of "It's HOW You Say It"™? You have the vision and you get the financials and all those other aspects of what you do. Take that vision a step further.

Let's take a look at how to BE the person you want others to think you already ARE. Leadership from the inside out means you must continue developing yourself throughout your career. Others will try to change you, but it is how you change yourself that counts. I believe there are five characteristics that identify a person as a true leader.

> *Fame is a vapor, popularity an accident, and riches take wings. Only one thing endures and that is character.*
> —*Horace Greeley, American newspaper editor, circa 1850s*

The Five Characteristics of a True Leader

1. Integrity
2. Compassion
3. Love
4. Faith
5. Generosity

1. Integrity

Integrity isn't an 8:00 - 5:00 corporate buzz word. Integrity is a verb, not literally, but figuratively. You live it. Not just at the office, not just in your home, but everywhere. On the road, with the cab driver, in negotiations, with the people you love and care about.

Integrity is not allowing the sales directors to hold sales a few days so they show up on the next month's numbers. Integrity is promoting the person you really don't care for because they truly are the best person for the job. Integrity is being a big enough person to help with the chores at home, letting your kids see that nobody is too important to help and everyone in the family pitches in and works together. Integrity is not trying to play word games so you don't feel guilty by saying the truth straight out. "I didn't lie. You asked if I liked and agreed with your proposal. I said, 'Yes.' I didn't say I was going to approve it."

> *The glue that holds all relationships together – including the relationship between the leader and the led is trust, and trust is based on integrity.*
> — **Brian Tracy, Motivational speaker, author, Chairman and CEO of Brian Tracy International**

Integrity has to do with your continuing executive skillset and having and building upon the knowledge and expertise that you espouse you have. Are you still current? When is the last time you acquired executive development? Many leaders get to a certain position and feel they have "arrived." Yet, when a train has arrived at its destination, the train is prepared for another journey to another destination. The engineer must learn new technology and new maps for a new environment, just as the leader must learn.

Are you connected to others at your position in other corporations? What direction is their company headed? What challenges are they facing as a leader (as a female leader, a male leader, a minority leader, etc.) in their industries? Are any of those similar to you?

Do you belong to a mastermind group with others in your position in your industry in other corporations? If you're not able to belong to a mastermind group with other leaders in your industry due to antitrust regulations, are you connected to a mastermind group across the country with people in like positions, and interests? What stimulates your thinking?

PART III   NAVIGATING THE STATIONS & SIDETRACKS TO REACH YOUR DESTINATION

What other stations could you carry this train to? What other corporations could help create synergies you may not even have thought of? How could you partner?

2. Compassion
Be Kind, Be Humble, Be Accepting, Be Gentle and Be Patient

> *If there is any great secret of success in life, it lies in the ability to put yourself in the other person's place and to see things*
> *from his point of view, as well as your own.*
> — **Henry Ford, industrialist**

Compassion - Would people in your company say that word fits you? When is the last time you left the executive offices and walked down the hall into the "train yard?" Do you treat employees all the same? Even if they are in the department or position from the "wrong side of the tracks?"

Many years ago, the leader I have spoken about treated everyone alike. We would meet on Monday mornings at the local coffee shop in the business park where our office was. As all the management walked over to get coffee on Monday mornings, this was a typical conversation to hear our executive area director, "Mr. Adams" [not his name] have with the grounds keepers and maintenance workers as we walked through the parking lot:

"Hi, Mr. Adams, how are you?"

"Hi, José, I'm well, how are you? How're your daughter's dance lessons going?"

"Oh, she still loves it, Mr. Adams. Thanks for asking."

"You bet, José, you must be awfully proud of her."

Everyone knew "Mr. Adams" and it seemed he knew something about every one of them, too.

In order for employers to build extraordinary leaders in their current teams, they first need to ensure they see each other as a team and not merely as individuals working together. There's a difference.

A team first has to agree on the values and goals of the team and, as important, hold each other accountable for demonstrating the values they've agreed upon on a day-to-day basis. When shareholder concerns weigh on a team, it's easier to ignore these values as just words on a plaque. A leader lives these values, at work and at home.

Many in leadership tend to be very analytical and rely heavily on the logical side of their experience and expertise than the human side. While these are good skills to have, the most important skill hasn't been exercised. The name of the children's game is Follow the Leader - not, follow the person in charge. Because you have a title, doesn't make you a leader. What does?

> *How do you develop extraordinary leaders?*
> *Develop first extraordinary people.*
> — **Barbara Teicher**

In theory, many leaders say they'd like to make a difference in their corporations, and in the world itself. A great leader makes a difference. DIFFERENCE. Look more closely at that word.

PART III   NAVIGATING THE STATIONS & SIDETRACKS TO REACH YOUR DESTINATION

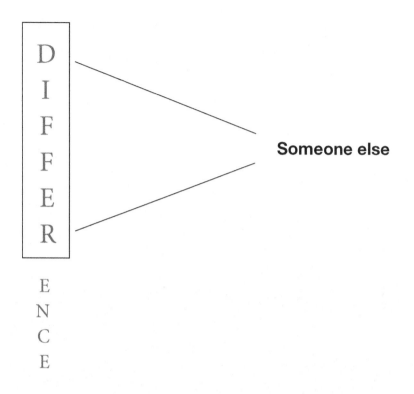

These same leaders think that to make a difference, it means they need to do something extraordinary, like solve world hunger or find a cure for cancer. That's overwhelming. So overwhelming, these same people DIFFER. They hand the responsibility for changing things for the better to others, to "someone else." The logical side of them says this is an overwhelming task that takes way too much time and energy. Time and energy they don't have. You may be the same way. As you look at the highlighted word, DIFFER, you may think, "Doesn't she know that the word she's actually referring to is DEFER and not DIFFER?" That's the point. We get stuck on details that keep us from getting to our ultimate goal. We do the proverbial "analysis paralysis." Nothing of consequence usually changes because of this. Then if you look at the word, differENCE, the end of it really says that if you defer, you are <u>E</u>vidently <u>N</u>ot <u>C</u>aring <u>E</u>nough.

D
I
F
F
E
R
E **EVIDENTLY**
N **NOT**
C **CARING**
E **ENOUGH**

To be a leader, you need to look at the impact of actions and human interactions, not merely the details of how to get to the finish line first.

Think about this. If you were gone from your company tomorrow, would it crumble? Hardly. We like to think it can't go on without us but that just isn't true. What legacy are you building, both at your company and in your personal life?

Remember the example of "Get Me Water" I shared in a previous chapter? The way the manager reacted to the crisis, and how they pushed that negative emotion back onto their direct report will have a lasting effect on that relationship. It will now become part of the employee's history with that manager next time they meet. The manager should have chosen to react the first time by showing a little compassion for the team member who was working hard too. They had rearranged their schedule to accommodate the manager's. Now, their future meetings will be starting off with unfinished emotional cargo still lingering.

Sometimes making a large DIFFERENCE can mean not getting off track yet making a big difference in the seemingly smallest of ways.

In his book *The Fred Factor*, by Mark Sanborn, Fred, a mail carrier, has a job that most people would see as nondescript and mundane. Do you know what your mail carrier looks like? Do you know their name?

According to Sanborn, "Some might see delivering mail as monotonous drudgery, but Fred sees the task as an opportunity to make the lives of his customers more enjoyable. Fred takes it upon himself to make a difference in the lives of the people he serves, even though he's "just" a mail carrier."

Remember, the name of the game is "Follow the Leader," not "Follow the Person in Charge." You don't have to have the title of leader, to be one.

3. Love

There are many definitions of this word. They are all along the same train-of-thought, yet all very different.

According to Webster's Dictionary, this is the primary definition of <u>love</u>:

It's HOW You Say It™

> ***LOVE* noun \ˈləv**
> ***a feeling of strong or constant affection for a person***

In the English language, we use the same word to describe a myriad of different emotions, all using the same word that have nothing to do with another person.

I love a great cup of coffee, I love to go out to lunch. I love what I do, I love going to the beach. All the same word.

What does LOVE have to do with being a great leader? If you look at the many books on love like *The Five Love Languages* by Gary Chapman, for instance, love isn't a noun. Love is a verb. To build or keep the feelings of love requires action. To be a great leader you must first be a great person and let others see that love through your day-to-day actions.

Love doesn't have to be about emotion. It can be about support and caring enough to put others before yourself. In order for people to feel you are a great leader, be a great person and let them see the care you have for others.

Do you have a housekeeper? Someone that cleans your home for you or does your laundry? Great! Are they a "hired servant" in your home, or someone you talk with often and know personally, too? Do you treat them as a friend? If I asked them myself, how would they say you treat them?

Matthew Butner - a True Story

Matthew Butner was on the fast track to success. In the early 1980's, someone believed in him and he went to work in Kansas City for the largest pharmaceutical company in town and one of the most respected in the country. The founder had

PART III   NAVIGATING THE STATIONS & SIDETRACKS TO REACH YOUR DESTINATION

a nationwide reputation for kindness, generosity and wildly successful business acumen.

The company grew by leaps and bounds and Matthew was picking up steam right along with it. He loved his work and he loved the company. By 2006 he was living around the world, staying several months in Berlin, moving on to France, jet-setting across Europe and North America. He was an Information Technology genius. He had responsibility for blending cross-functional world-wide teams, and consulted with numerous executives across the board on multimillion dollar Information Technology projects. With this responsibility came all the visibility, prestige and financial rewards that you would expect. His train had arrived. As the company grew, it acquired other companies and continued to chug toward global recognition.

While everyone has setbacks, Matthew had a few side tracks as well. The company was being purchased by a large conglomerate out of France. Matthew was responsible for leading the team that would, ultimately, consolidate his team into the new company and move the headquarters to France. Matthew knew this was the right thing for the company's success and supported it as strongly as any other project he'd done.

Matthew started a new train of thought. He wondered if it was time to slow down. He realized he was missing his wife and that his kids were getting to the age where he'd be missing time, like the coach in an earlier example, that he'd never get back. Matthew had a love for his company, yet a strong love for his family.

Matthew noticed during this time that although he worked out faithfully, he was starting to lift less weight and feel more fatigue. His arm strength started to deteriorate until he couldn't ignore it and sought help. He was told he had ALS, a fatal neuromuscular disease. His doctors said he had six months to live. A person's priorities and what their TRUE loves are must come screaming into focus when being derailed with that kind of news.

Being dedicated to all the loves in his life, Matthew tried to hide this from his work. He had a trusted friend at the office who would help him put on and button his coat. All the things most people take for granted, he was now struggling with.

If you were to describe Matthew, the first words you would think of are love, service and passion. Love and passion for his work, his teams, his family and his purpose and service to those same people.

I asked him what some of the lessons learned were from his illness and what contributed to his wild success during those years. He told me ensuring the success of the teams led to his success. He always put them first, helped them succeed, genuinely enjoyed their company and never forgot where he started.

> *My door was always open, and the candy jar full. [The founder of the company] taught me the value of putting others first... The minute I stopped worrying about climbing the ladder is when it all came to me.*
> —Matthew Butner

> *Love is something you do for someone else, not something you do for yourself.*
> —Gary Chapman, *The Five Love Languages, Singles Edition*

The corporation has a yearly award pursued by all team members. This is an international award with significant impact. The entire corporation's team members covet it. The year Matthew was leaving the company, this honor was bestowed upon him. With all the wonderful things happening by wonderful people across the globe, the one person who won it was Matthew.

What's even more significant is that award was given to an employee they had already terminated. The award was freely given by the leadership of the French corporation, to an American. You see, Matthew was as much loved in Europe, as he was in America. Quite an accomplishment.

Although Matthew has beaten the odds to this point, he is now aware his disease is a rare form of ALS. Currently, among five neurologists, three say this disease will continue to cause degeneration and will end his life within two years. Two say, although degenerative, he could live to be 90. He's going with their diagnosis.

Matthew is now in the private sector enjoying and loving his family, friends and sharing his lessons learned.

For more information on Matthew and his story, please contact...

Matthew Butner
Lionheart Transitions
Matthew@mjbLion.com
www.mjbLion.com
816-564-2482

People still relate to people on a human level first. Just be real. It's okay to laugh at yourself when you make a mistake.

Know that other people are laughing whether you do or not! Being more "real" makes you more relatable as a leader.

Make your priorities to support and serve those family and friends, those in the corporation and in the community that keep life and business running smoothly across those tracks.

Know too, that if you leave the ivory tower to meet and greet the teams to start building relationships, you may see light at the end of the tunnel, but it may be a train! Don't expect to be shown a shower of love and gratitude when you go out because of your position. Respect is earned, over time, slowly and steadily.

Love is a verb. Talk is cheap. How are you demonstrating that you are capable of loving someone besides yourself? Loving is serving. Love is BEING the person you want others to think you already ARE.

Are there people you need to say "I love you" to? That could be verbally, it could be through your actions or it could be through your support. Does it matter if they are a husband, wife, brother, sister, in-law, or outlaw? What about co-workers at the office? If you aren't speaking now, do you remember why? Does it really matter who apologizes first?

> *I am amazed by how many individuals mess up every new day with yesterday.*
> —Gary Chapman Author of *Five Love Languages*

A best friend of mine in the Chicago area lost her husband suddenly this year two days before Christmas. He just, died. It was totally unexpected. They have two sons. One still in high school. So many things she wished she had said, done, shown.

PART III   NAVIGATING THE STATIONS & SIDETRACKS TO REACH YOUR DESTINATION

> *Love doesn't erase the past,
> but it makes the future different.*
> —Gary Chapman Author of *Five Love Languages*

How do leaders LOVE?

L - Live
O - Our
V - Values
E - Everywhere, Everyday

Think back to when you were little and growing up in grade school, even high school. Think about the people who you admired. Who were your heroes (or SHEroes)? Why did you admire them? What was it about them that you were drawn to, made you feel special or made you feel they were special?

Take a minute to think about that. In the blanks below, think of three words that really describe those people and what you most admired, what made the relationship special.

1. _____

2. _____

3. _____

If I had your direct reports, your peers and your most senior leadership in a room with me, privately, one at a time, what words would they use to describe you?

Look at your list above. Were any of the three words that defined the people you admired most growing up, words they would use to describe you? If not, why not?

A good leader knows who to give certain tasks to. That's important. HOW you delegate those tasks and responsibilities out, the way you say it, that's where the love comes in. Having a spirit of love doesn't mean you let people walk on you. You don't need to come across as weak. Just the opposite. Be self-assured. However, remember that delegation doesn't mean domination. That's important.

4. Faith

Faith may sound like an unusual step to leadership.

> *Leadership should be as much about your journey as a person as it is a destination to your career.*
> — Barbara Teicher

Where do you think you came from? How do you think we all got here? More importantly, where do you think you're going?

What is faith? Do you have it? What does it have to do with leadership? If you do have a faith, would people know your faith by how you live your life, or is it something that slips into your calendar once a week and then you're finished with it until you "have to" go to a church or synagogue again?

Many people have a need to be in control. Faith is a very difficult concept because it means relinquishing your control

PART III NAVIGATING THE STATIONS & SIDETRACKS TO REACH YOUR DESTINATION

to a higher power. Most people who love to control situations aren't willing to give up that power. It really is a moot point though. No matter how powerful we think we are, there will always be someone who has more. No matter who has more, The Supreme being, creator of the universe, will always be at the top of that food chain. In my faith, I call that supreme power God.

Some people may say they don't believe in God. That too is a moot point. Early settlers may not have believed the Earth was round. Because they didn't believe it, didn't mean it wasn't so.

Ultimately, faith is knowing we don't have to carry the weight of the world (the corporation, the family, the finances, etc.) all alone on our own shoulders. Faith is not a religion or a church building, it's not a list of do's and don'ts. Faith is the personal relationship you have with your Creator.

So, why is faith an integral step in becoming a strong, effective leader? It doesn't mean you need to share with people what your faith is at the office. The point of this isn't to support one religion over another. The point is that all of us, to achieve greatness, need to relinquish the fact that we don't hold a candle to what true greatness is.

The skills described and taught in earlier chapters of this book mean nothing without the leader having a strong set of values that guides his/her life. I believe my faith helps to shape who I am and drives the type of leader I have become.

The Background

When I was very young, I thought my family was like any other family. If you're old enough to remember this, I felt like we could be "The Waltons." As I got older, I realized that wasn't the case at all.

In our family, there are four girls and a boy. My brother is right in the middle in age, and I'm the baby. We did things most families do. We went on summer vacations, went to the park, and we went to church every Sunday at 9:00. We had to go at 9:00 not 11:00. For some reason I think my dad thought if you went to mass earlier, it meant you were holier, or something. All of us had also, through the years, attended the church school.

What I realized is that although we went to church, and to the school, we didn't really know about or have an actual relationship with God. We went to church, we were seen and we followed the rules. No meat on Friday, go to church on Sunday, give some money. If you grew up in a similar situation, you're probably aware of what I'm talking about.

That's all we were supposed to "do," right? I didn't really understand any of it, didn't really know God and had no idea what His teachings actually were. It boils down to this. There are people who SAY they are people of faith and people who LIVE like people of faith. That's totally different too. For instance, you can say you love seafood. But if you don't ever order it, turn it down when it's offered to you, won't go to restaurants that specialize in it, talk is cheap.

When you have a faith relationship, you try to live the kind of life God wants you to live. Don't get me wrong, nobody's perfect. We can't be either. That's why as part of this relationship, you're forgiven. This is not about getting you to attend my place of worship. As a leader, what you should care about is becoming more of the person you want to truly be. The values of faith are your light at the end of the tunnel, your switching station to keep you on the right track and your signals to help you know what to turn toward and what to turn away from.

PART III   NAVIGATING THE STATIONS & SIDETRACKS TO REACH YOUR DESTINATION

How I Found My Faith

Through many years I realized, my dad had issues I never knew. They have affected my sisters to this day. My mom had mental illness. I was home during her first episode and she ultimately committed suicide when I was 25. That was a difficult time for me. I smoked and drank and thought everyone else should too.

Then, several years later, my room mate, and close, close friend died. She was 29 years old. She died in her sleep. Her name was Debbie. I am the one who found her. It was, to say the least, the most traumatic time in my life. After that, I was angry at the world. She was 29, she didn't do drugs, didn't really drink, it wasn't fair. Life wasn't fair.

I remember sitting on the floor of our apartment after the funeral, all alone in the middle of the afternoon. I was crying and angry. I screamed out, "If there's a God, where ARE you!? What do you want from me? You took my mother, you took my room mate. If you're really there, I need you. Prove it!"

No more than half an hour later, my phone rang. It was my brother on the other side of the state. He told me he had spoken to my sister-in-law, and they thought I should leave where I was to move and come live with them. (I had just turned thirty two months before.) Thirty minutes. Cool.

"What about my job?"

"You hate it. You're working in a restaurant." Good point.

"What about my boyfriend?"

"You don't want to keep seeing him. He's an idiot." They were two for two.

So I moved.

They say coincidence is God's way of remaining anonymous. When I finally sought Him, He showed up. He didn't push His way into my life. He waited until He was invited.

That day changed my life. I moved, got a great, new job with a wonderful company and several months after I moved to my own apartment, I got "Saved."

Does this mean you'll get a phone call in thirty minutes that will change your life? Maybe not. But if you "call" for Him, He will answer.

My faith is the guiding factor of my life. It gives me strength, helps guide decisions, gives me a quiet peace and helps a smile glow in my heart. I'll admit, some days the smile may shine brighter than others. I'm human! My values are based on my faith knowing that God is with me. Those values guide my leadership decisions and interactions and provide focus. Where do your values come from? What are they based on? Are you carrying the stress of the company as well?If you are trying to guide and make all the decisions in your life on your own, I believe you are headed for a train wreck.

5. Generosity

It would be much easier if I would say generosity were all about money. For most people in higher leadership positions, giving money to charities isn't difficult. It checks the box of "done that" when we know we should give back.

Generosity is much more than that. Generosity is giving of your time when that direct report comes in and asks, for the third time, the question you feel you've answered at least that many times already. Do you volunteer for a charity, church or civic organization with those less fortunate than you? Or do you revert to what we talked about earlier in the chapter and leave that for "someone else" to make that difference?

Many people that work in large corporations love to give to the yearly corporate charity drive. Don't get me wrong, that's a worthy organization. You can check the box, they can take donations right out of your paycheck and your conscience is clear, right?

True generosity means going that extra mile. Do you do anything else to give back? Do you offer your time volunteering with that or other organizations? Are you on the board of any of these organizations? Are you generous with your time at your company? Do you mentor any staff or have skip-level meetings? A skip-level meeting doesn't include mid-level managers. You "skip" their participation and make it directly an open forum meeting with the employees and leadership. These are meant to be in a safe environment. The purpose is to share feedback confidentially without fear of your manager being in the room. It's also a chance for leadership to see how everyone is. Do you ever take a cup of coffee or tea and just walk around in the morning to say, "Hi."

Do you give your time at home? Sometimes, when we get home, the last thing we want to do is go out again. Has someone there been stuck in the house all day? Do you offer to go out? If you live with others, are you generous in supporting the home? Taking out the trash, cleaning, or just sitting on the couch and talking? Generosity is only partly about financials.

You've heard the saying, "It's better to give than to receive." So g-i-v-e.

It's HOW You Say It™

How Generous are you?

Directions: Answer each question Yes or No. Record the point value listed for each "Yes" answer.

Activity	Yes	No	Points Value	Your Points
Do you give to a charitable organization through work?			1	
Do you give to a church or synagogue?			1	
If your answer directly above is yes, add an extra point if those donations are above your giving through work.			1	
Do you volunteer your time with charitable organizations through work (painting homes, etc)?			2	
If you answered yes above add a point if you do it more than once per year.			1	
Are you a mentor? If yes, do you meet at least monthly?			2	
Do you regularly volunteer your time with organizations and charities outside work?			3	
Are you on an active committee with them? (Give yourself 3 points for each active committee you participate on)			3	
Are you a member of the board of a charitable or civic organization?			3	
At least once per month do you bring dinner or run errands for someone outside your family as an act of kindness?			3	
Your Point Totals				

Here's what the point scale represented:
0 = None
1 = Good start
2 = You give back through work
3 = You are making a difference

Let's Check Your Score

Number of Points Earned

15 - 20+	Congratulations. You are generous with your talents and resources. You are making an impact and a strong difference in your community.
10 - 14	You are on the right track. Look for small opportunities to help that could make a big difference.
5 - 10	You are aware you should give back. That's great. You've started although haven't made volunteering and giving back a priority yet.
< 5	What kind of person do you want to truly be? Re-evaluate ways you can become involved to make a difference. Don't rely only on the list above. Please don't wait for "someone else" to do these things.

The Science of It All

In *Lifelong Health,* Dr. David Lipschitz reports that, in recent years, the discussion of faith and health has worked its way into the mainstream. Research has shown that those who believe in a higher power, attend religious services frequently and pray regularly tend to live longer, are less likely to be depressed, have a lower risk of and recover more quickly from illness and have fewer complications.

Studies have shown that when a social worker makes a visit to a patient and discusses issues of faith and provides spiritual support, the patient responds better to therapy, hospital stays are reduced and costs of care decrease. The evidence linking faith to better health is far from definitive, but compelling nonetheless.

Closely related to faith, are the values we discussed earlier in the chapter: love, compassion and caring. Do they really have a place in a fast-paced environment focused on financials?

Let's take these values and one last look at the research project by the Harvard Business School Professors James Heskett and John Kotter and compare the two. You'll remember what they focused on was not just the revenues of the companies, the focus rather was on the cultures, the actual values, of these corporations. They wanted to see how the company's corporate internal culture impacted its economic performance over a long period of time. Their book I've mentioned, *Corporate Culture and Performance*, argued that companies and corporations that had a strong culture that could quickly change and adapt to the changing world around them were linked to strong financial results. What's more interesting is that they placed a very high value on their employees (love), as well as their customers and the owners (caring). They sincerely encouraged leadership from everyone in the company. The benefit was that as a customer's need changed, as they often do, employees were empowered to do what was right for the customer (faith values/compassion/generosity). That may mean changing a practice or policy, if warranted. Every employee in the company was empowered to do that.

PART III   NAVIGATING THE STATIONS & SIDETRACKS TO REACH YOUR DESTINATION

All Aboard

Take these two steps:

1. Write Your Personal Life's Belief Statement.

Make time for one of the most important trips you'll ever plan: The rest of your life. This is not a journey with a physical location destination.

Think about the different tracks in your life: Family, career, friends, health, faith, giving. Who are you now, and who is it you truly, down beneath the stage lights, want to be? How do you want others to perceive who you are and the life you lead? How will that perception be reality?

This is not about money, possessions, power, prestige or image. It is about the definition of your life and who you are as a person when no one is watching. What's important to you? Where are you now on those tracks and what actions will help drive you to your ultimate destination?

Is it time for you to switch tracks? Are there cars of past baggage you need to disconnect from and make a fresh start? Do you need to offer forgiveness to someone, even if you feel you were in the right? Do you need to go back, mend some things and make changes before you can chug ahead? Sometimes, the biggest step in moving forward is to first, move back.

> *We all want progress, but if you're on the wrong road, progress means doing an about turn and walking back to the right road. In that case, the man who turns back soonest is the most progressive.*
>
> — C.S. Lewis

2. Join a Mastermind Group.

Connect with people in similar positions within similar industries. Go on the internet and search out people in like corporations or companies, research them, see what organizations they are in. Reach out to them, introduce yourself and ask if they would be interested in connecting for 30 minutes. If you feel they have similar values and focus, conference once every quarter. If they don't, move on to another contact. Let them help you expand your knowledge into their world. Help them do the same with yours. If your positions are similar, and they are in similarly sized companies, your challenges and issues will be similar, as well.

Do you have a faith you practice? Is it time to reconnect?

Remember, it's not the destination that's important, it's the journey to get there (Ralph Waldo Emerson is attributed for this quote).

Take time in a quiet place in your home or outside in a natural setting, somewhere you can be alone, not disturbed and have at least thirty minutes to think. Look at the steps to leadership below that were discussed in this chapter. Think about where you are in these areas:

1. Integrity
2. Compassion
3. Love
4. Faith
5. Generosity

PART III NAVIGATING THE STATIONS & SIDETRACKS TO REACH YOUR DESTINATION

Now think about where you want to be. WHO you want to be. What values do you want to drive your life? What is your faith? Write your life's Belief Statement. Take time with this. It doesn't have to be long, one or two paragraphs that describe the future state of the person you want to BE.

Keep this statement with you in your wallet or at your desk. Tape it to your mirror. Every day, read it before you head out. Every night, as you give thanks for the day, for your blessings, for the people you value most in your life, think about an example of one thing you did that day that is a demonstration of the person you are moving closer towards becoming.

> *What counts in life is not the mere fact that we have lived. It is what difference we have made to the lives of others that will determine the significance of the life we lead.*
> **Nelson Mandela** *(1918 - 2013) South African anti-apartheid revolutionary, politician, and philanthropist. President of South Africa from 1994 to 1999*

ALL ABOARD!

Summary

As you move through this wild ride called life, remember at the heart of it all is just that: your heart. The Five Characteristics of a True Leader aren't just for the people who have a corporate leadership title. Leadership is a mindset and the skills for leadership can be taught. Practicing the skills and principles in this book— making a V.A.S.T. difference in your workplace, your neighborhoods and your communities, striving to treat people how you, and they, would like to be treated, continuing to learn and improve your subject matter knowledge and expertise, and conducting yourself and your life, in such a way that makes you proud to be who you are—is what will make you a true leader.

About the Author

As you get to know Barbara Teicher, you will immediately see that she has taken her nearly 6' height to the level that reaches her skills and experiences as a keynote speaker, author, corporate trainer, and coach.

Barbara guides her audiences in a lighthearted look at the reasons for challenges they face in business communications and interactions with customers and employees. She brings common sense to all this with a no-nonsense approach to changing difficult situations into lasting solutions.

Ms. Teicher brings her 25-plus years of developing leaders in Fortune 50-500 companies to every engagement and forum in which she works. She specializes in effective business communication and leadership development. Barbara has appeared on the NBC affiliate "Kansas City Live" to showcase a state-of-the-art executive briefing center and has delivered presentations on advanced business solutions to senior officers of the most recognized brands in the world.

...It's HOW You Say It™

Barbara consulted on and critiqued an executive simulation conducted at the University of Pennsylvania's Wharton School of Business. She is the 2014-2015 president of the National Speakers Association's Kansas City chapter, a member of the Global Speaker's Federation and a mentor for MBA and EMBA students with the Helzberg School of Management at Rockhurst University. She is the winner of Action Management Associates "Million Dollar Award."

Barbara lives in the Kansas City area with her husband, Adam, and their rambunctious dog Aspen. She and her husband are the proud parents of an honors college sophmore daughter at Colorado State University.

You will learn quickly she adds life to her company motto and belief "It's HOW You Say It."™

...It's HOW You Say It℠

Barbara Teicher

etc.

Executive Training and Coaching

Corporate Training • Coaching • **Motivational Speaking** • Seminars & Workshops

Phone 913-707-5826   Barbara@ItsHowYouSayIt.com   www.ItsHowYouSayIt.com

To Order

To order additional copies of this book, please go to www.Amazon.com

To have Barbara speak at your conference or convention, or for additional information on corporate training, products and services, please contact (913) 707-5826 or send inquiries to Info@ItsHOWYouSayIt.com.

If you feel it may be time to investigate this mystery called faith and reinforce this track in your life, or if you have a curiosity about what a relationship with God could be, contact a local church in your area. There are many different types of services from the very traditional to contemporary. Find the one that speaks to wonderful you.

Resources

Ronald B. Adler and Jeanne Marquardt Elmhorst. *Communicating at Work: Principles and Practices for Business and the Professions.* Boston: McGraw Hill, 2002.

Karen Anderson. *Making Meetings Work: How to Plan and Conduct Effective Meetings.* West Des Moines, IA: American Media Publishing, 1999.

Anne Baber and Lynne Waymon. *Make Your Contacts Count: Networking Know-how for Business and Career Success.* NY: Amacon, 2007.

Fernando Bartolome. *"Nobody Trusts the Boss Completely—Now What?"* Harvard Business Review, originally published in 1989.

Kenneth H. Blanchard. *Situational Leadership II.* Blanchard Training and Development, Inc. (published article), 1994.

Dianna Booher. *Communicate with Confidence! How to Say It Right the First Time and Every Time.* NY: McGraw Hill, 1994.

Joe Calhoun. "Business Values: What Standards Help Your Team Work Together and Actually Enjoy Doing It." Training program, 2013.

John S. Caputo, Harry C. Hazel, and Colleen McMahon. *Interpersonal Communication: Competency through Critical Thinking.* Boston: Allyn and Bacon, 1994.

David Caruso and Peter Salovey. *The Emotionally Intelligent Manager: How to Develop and Use the Four Key Emotional Skills of Leadership.* 2004.

Gary D. Chapman. *The Five Love Languages: The Secret to Love That Lasts.* NY: Moody Publishers, 2009.

Robert A. Cialdini. "Harnessing the Science of Persuasion." *Harvard Business Review.* 2001.

David A. Garvin and Michael A. Roberto. "What You Don't Know about Making Decisions." *Harvard Business Review.* 2001.

Connie Glaser. *GenderTalk Works: 7 Steps for Cracking the Gender Code.* Windsor Hall Press, 2007.

Daniel Goleman. *Emotional Intelligence: Why It Can Matter More Than IQ.* NY: Bantam Books, 2005.

Daniel Goleman. *Social Intelligence: The New Science of Human Relationships.* NY: Banta Books, 2007.

Daniel Goleman. *Understanding the Science of Moods at Work.* To be published in 2014.

John Gray. *Men Are from Mars, Women Are from Venus: The Classic Guide to Understanding the Opposite Sex.* NY: HarperCollins, 1992.

Horace Greeley. www.tulane.edu/~latner/Greeley.html

Edward T. Hall. *The Silent Language.* NY: Harcourt, 1959.

Harvard Business Review on Effective Communication. Boston: Harvard Business School Press, 1999.

Harvard Business Review on the Persuasive Leader. Boston: Harvard Business Press. 2008.

Angela Haupt. "How to Forgive and Why You Should." *US News & World Report.* 29 Aug. 2012.

Susan C. Herring. "Who's Got the Floor in Computer-mediated Conversation? Edelsky's Gender Patterns Revisited." Language@Internet, 7, article 8. 2010.

Sam Horn. *Tongue Fu! ® How to Deflect, Disarm, and Defuse Any Verbal Conflict.* NY:

St. Martin's Press, 1996.

John P. Kotter and James L. Heskett. *Corporate Culture and Performance*. NY: Free Press, 1992.

David Lipschitz. *Lifelong Health*. www.arcamax.com

Michael Maccoby. "Why People Follow the Leader: The Power of Transference." *Harvard Business Review*. 2004.

Nelson Mandela. *Long Walk to Freedom: The Autobiography of Nelson Mandela*. NY: Little, Brown and Co., 1993.

Louise H. Marshall and Horace W. Magoun. *Discoveries in the Human Brain: Neuroscience Prehistory, Brain Structure, and Function*. Totowa, NJ: Humana Press, 1998.

John C. Maxwell. *The 21 Irrefutable Laws of Leadership: Follow Them and People Will Follow You*. Nashville: Thomas Nelson, 2007.

Albert Mehrabian. *Silent Messages: Implicit Communication of Emotions and Attitudes*. Belmont, CA: Wadsworth, 1981.

Hawk Nelson. "Words" (song).

Ralph G. Nichols and Leonard A. Stevens. "Listening to People." Harvard Business Review, originally published in 1957.

Alex (Sandy) Pentland. *Honest Signals: How They Shape Our World*. Cambridge, MA: MIT Press, 2008.

Alex (Sandy) Pentland. *Social Physics: How Good Ideas Spread—The Lessons from a New Science*. NY: Penguin Press, 2014.

Donald T. Phillips. *Lincoln on Leadership: Executive Strategies for Tough Times*. NY: Business Plus, 1992.

Watty Piper (a.k.a. Arnold Munk). *The Little Engine that Could*.1930.

Marcia Purse. *What's in a Smile? Expression Affects Emotion*. Blog. www.healthcentral/profile/c/687619, 2013.

David Rock. *Your Brain at Work: Strategies for Overcoming Distractions, Regaining Focus, and Working Smarter All Day Long.* NY: HarperCollins Publishing, 2009.

Lesley Roger. *Sexing the Brain.* NY: Columbia University Press, 2001.

Mark Sanborn. *The Fred Factor: How Passion in Your Work and Life Can Turn the Ordinary into the Extraordinary.* NY: Random House, 2008.

Mark Sanborn. *Fred 2.0: New Ideas on How to Keep Delivering Extraordinary Results.* Carol Stream, IL: Tyndale House Publishers, 2013.

David Snowden. *Aging with Grace: What the Nun Study Teaches Us about Leading Longer, Healthier, and More Meaningful Lives.* NY: Bantam Books, 2001.

Deborah Tannen. *That's Not What I Meant!: How Conversational Style Makes or Breaks Relationships.* NY: HarperCollins, 2011.

Deborah Tannen. *You Just Don't Understand: Women and Men in Conversation.* NY: William Marrow, 1990.

John V. Thill and Courtland L. Bovee. *Excellence in Business Communication.* NY: Prentice Hall, 2011.

Brian Tracy. www.briantracy.com

Rick Warren. *The Purpose Driven Life: What on Earth Am I Here for?* Grand Rapids, WI: Zondervan, 2002.

Bowen F. White. Why Normal Isn't Reality: How to Find Heart, Meaning, Passion and Humor on the Road Most Traveled. Stress Technologies, 2004.

Made in the USA
Monee, IL
23 March 2023